HELLO KEW

For Valentine: a wish when I started
writing this book; a real, living boy
by the time I had finished.

HELLO KEW

A souvenir scrapbook

SOPHIE SHILLITO

Kew Publishing
Royal Botanic Gardens, Kew

First published in 2023 by
Royal Botanic Gardens, Kew,
Richmond, Surrey, TW9 3AB, UK
www.kew.org

ISBN 978 1 84246 780 0

Distributed on behalf of the Royal Botanic Gardens, Kew in North America
by the University of Chicago Press, 1427 East 60th St, Chicago, IL 60637, USA.

British Library Cataloguing in Publication Data
A catalogue record for this book is available from the British Library

DESIGN: Kevin Knight
PRODUCTION MANAGER: Georgie Hills
TYPESETTING AND PAGE LAYOUT: Christine Beard
COPY-EDITING: Ellen Reid
PROOFREADING: Matthew Seal

Printed and bound in the UK by Gomer Press Limited

The guidebooks, postcards and other visual and written material are from the author's own collection and Kew's Library, Art and Archives. Every effort has been made to contact the copyright holders, and the Royal Botanic Gardens, Kew apologises for any unintentional errors or omissions, which will be corrected in future editions of this book. Please get in contact at publishing@kew.org.

For information or to purchase all Kew titles please visit
shop.kew.org/kewbooksonline or email publishing@kew.org

Kew's mission is to understand and protect plants and fungi, for the wellbeing of people and the future of all life on Earth.

Kew receives approximately one third of its funding from Government through the Department for Environment, Food and Rural Affairs (Defra). All other funding needed to support Kew's vital work comes from members, foundations, donors and commercial activities, including book sales.

CONTENTS

PREFACE

Collecting

A couple of years ago, curious about the Gardens' historic landscape, I bought a cheap, second-hand copy of Kew's 1951 guidebook. The apple-green volume cost just a couple of pounds, but the value of the object I held in my hands was immeasurable. I was instantly hooked. Human beings are collectors of things, and I am no exception. One guidebook wasn't enough, and quickly I hunted down other editions published throughout the 19th and 20th centuries.

For days, I pored over them. Some of the titles alone are fabulous, such as 1858's *Museum of Economic Botany Or A Popular Guide To The Useful And Remarkable Vegetable Products In The Two Museum Buildings Of The Royal Gardens of Kew*, and the 1912 *Popular Official Guide To The Royal Botanic Gardens Including An Historic Notice And Descriptions Of The Collections In The Botanic Gardens Proper, The Glass Houses, Museums And Arboretum*.

The language used on the covers continues with the same floridity on the pages within; as the many quotes used in this book demonstrate, the guidebook authors often had a dreamy facility with words, describing the Gardens with incredibly romantic turns of phrase. The Rhododendron Dell, for example, is a "winding valley", irises are "beautiful lavender-blue" and the plants in the Palm House are described as possessing "various tints of verdure". For your reading pleasure, I have collected the most beautiful, funny and eccentric original guidebook text and curated it within the pages of this book – you can find it italicised in each chapter.

I frittered hours admiring the artistic design of the guidebooks: the earliest editions are often illustrated with intricate drawings of plants growing in the glasshouses and the striking architecture found in Kew's landscape, and by the mid-1900s blooming bushes and stunning views were captured in gloriously vivid polychrome photographs. The colour pallets used on the covers and the flyleaf designs are aesthetically appealing; endpapers often include intriguing adverts for ultramodern mowers, hedge trimmers, gardening books and camera film with which to snap happy memories.

For a long time, I studied the detailed fold-out maps, thinking about the wild places marked inside their regimented squares; tracing my finger along vistas drawn in black and white, using the glasshouses and follies to guide me, crow-like, looking at how the landscape has both changed and stayed the same. These maps are treasure maps — they tell me things about the Gardens' past that I can no longer see in the landscape.

Snipping and sticking

Like every collector of things, I felt the inexplicable pull of the objects which I had gathered together. Touching the books, holding them in my hands, feeling their soft, worn pages and inhaling that warm smell of history thrilled me. The guidebooks became found objects, a library of curiosities that I wanted to share. I photographed them, and copied out passages, collecting fragments of beautiful, meaningful language in my notebooks. I began using parts of the guidebooks in my own collage, trying to tell the story of the Gardens over time.

I have created this book by weaving together snippets of old guidebooks and new writing. Like a gardener chops at a shrubbery, I have clipped out pieces of Kew from musty guidebook pages and pasted them into a new whole — bending trees and water, gluing together old stone and brick to fashion a scrapbook

stuffed with words and pictures. Kew itself is, after all, a scrapbook of a garden —
a patchwork of different landscapes, a mosaic of enamelled green jewels. Most of
Kew's collage can still be seen today, but some of it lies buried deep, in both the
earth and collective memory.

Time-travelling

Much of Kew's patchwork nature is formed not only from the many unique
gardens which compose its greater whole, but also, and perhaps more
significantly, from the different landscape layers that fold over one another to
create the history of the Gardens. Kew is a palimpsest — look carefully and the
past can be glimpsed in the reflections on the Pond; it lurks down in the woods
at the edge of the river; it broods amongst the Rhododendrons, deep in the Dell,
where the soil smells dank and leafy. At Kew, history is everywhere.

Kew is a time-worn tapestry: woven from different strands, patched, mended
and changed over centuries. Like a scarred body, the beauty of the land lies in
its imperfections, it is transformed through incident, altered and made through
its past; a past inextricably related to human activity — people have known and
visited the land at Kew for centuries.

Photograph taken in the early 1900s showing visitors around the Refreshment Pavilion.

Before the royal family founded their estate at Kew, the land was a wilderness; scrubby woodland and brush scrawled across an ancient valley carved out by a wide, wild river which dragged sticks and soil inside itself as it flowed seaward, making marshes and swampy pools. The landscape that the monarchy first knew was still partly covered with thick forest, through which pathways wound, slithering their way through shadowy labyrinths; birds and animals made their homes in bramble bushes that snarled over heathland. Later, the marshes became watermeadows where cattle and sheep grazed; in the King's fields, a golden harvest of corn, oats and barley grew.

Eventually, as lawns were seeded, flowers planted and hillocks formed from old, cold mud, the Kew landscape that we know today began to take shape. Glorious architectural follies sprouted from the soil, tiny saplings were planted and grew into the wizened giants we now picnic beneath. As the land passed from royal to governmental jurisdiction, new buildings and glasshouses were constructed, soil was scooped to make beautiful pools, and intriguing new plants were made to feel at home. Kew welcomed new visitors, too, and introduced them to its layered landscape through the medium of the guidebook, allowing them to understand the complex history of the land through which they walked.

Here, I have tried to create a composite compendium of the many changing impressions of Kew captured in its guidebooks over centuries. This book is a time-traveller's guide to Kew, where some features in the landscape that never existed at the same time can be understood in the space of a few paragraphs. Look amongst the pages for history's soily strata, elderly trees, demolished buildings, and shadowy avenues where thousands of feet have walked before. Think of it as a keepsake from history, a souvenir from a trip to a time before ours, a way of remembering the past glory of Kew, and all the people who visited the Gardens.

Discovering and imagining

Many excellent books covering Kew's large, historical events have been written, and whilst I have relied on these as part of my research, I have no desire to produce another. I am much more interested in revealing the more personal, human, intimate details from Kew's past; smaller things that I have discovered by studying the fascinating journals, records and ephemera in Kew's archives, moments that may have been forgotten: the name of the man who looked after the horses; the sound of the bell that called the gardeners to work; the words in the handwritten letter that inspired a new building; the taste of the sticky buns on the refreshment menu.

Kew's guidebooks are a portal to the past, allowing us to slip through history. Reading them, looking at the drawings and photographs, is akin to time-travel. Deep in their pages, I enter a liminal space, where the words I am reading inspire my imagination — I can almost walk in the historical Gardens, my footprints leaving no trace on the lawn as I watch royal courtiers take picnics down to Queen Charlotte's Cottage for the King and Queen to feast on; I watch across the water as Museum Number One is built on the far side of the Pond; I hear long-dead gardeners washing the windows of the Orchid House, whistling as they work.

At the beginning of each chapter, I have taken historical fact and twisted my imagination around it, conjuring moments from Kew's history, reanimating them with new words. Like the fantastical Kylins that guard the Pond, this book is a chimera — a mixture of fact, poetry, pictures and history, a palimpsestic treasury, a story that captures Kew's spirit of place.

Spirit of place

Kew's guidebooks, of course, would not exist without Kew — if there were no landscape to decipher, no words would be written about it; if the Gardens never were, there would be no need to describe and interpret them.

Much of the writing in the guidebooks can be thought of as place writing: words that aim to capture the landscape's quintessence. I have tried to do the same in this book, distilling Kew's spirit, to make a pure concentrate that embodies the land and everything it encapsulates.

Kew is composed of many different textures and fabrics — the river, the trees, the buildings, the earth, the plants — and it is not solely one of these things that speaks of the landscape, but rather their combined whole. It is Kew's inimitable mixture of grand vistas, woodland walks, deep water and shimmering glass that makes it Kew; and yet it is more than these things also — it is the colour, light and movement that are singularly peculiar to Kew, that are unique to this particular, special place on Earth, a place unlike any other.

When I was researching this book, I walked in the Gardens almost every day.

When you visit the same landscape often, you begin to know it. Knowing a place is like knowing a person; there is an intimacy, an understanding. Kew is more than a garden to me — it is the feeling of an old friend; it is the sanctuary of home. Kew is alive: it has a soul and a distinctive atmosphere which I have tried to capture in these pages.

Welcome to Kew

I hope you will use this book as a Gardens' gazetteer — a handbook, a manual with which to explore and discover Kew. As you do, take your own pictures, write down your thoughts, make your own scrapbook of memories.

Your visit to Kew, however brief, will alter it. Strands of your hair will be made into a bird's nest, your breath will help a tree to grow, your footsteps will dimple the land. You will mark Kew in the same way it marks you, and you will leave part of yourself behind so your story is woven into the landscape, too.

Floreat Kew! May Kew Flourish!

Sophie Shillito
January 2023

The Rhododendron Dell, Kew Gardens.

13108

INTRODUCTION

A SHORT HISTORY
OF VISITING KEW

A central theme of this book is the experience of visiting Kew. Visiting gardens is a national preoccupation for the British, and Kew can be considered the country's unofficial national garden. A visit to Kew can indeed be thought of as a secular pilgrimage; a special journey to a sacred place of great historical, architectural and botanical importance.

Visiting gardens for pleasure has been a leisure activity for the wealthy for hundreds of years, and Kew is no exception. As Ray Desmond explains in *The History of the Royal Botanic Gardens, Kew,* his canonical text about the Gardens, in the 1700s "earnest tourists, assiduously visiting country houses and their gardens, usually included ... Kew in their itinerary". And for the less pecunious too, visiting gardens became ever more popular as days off and holiday time increased. In the 1800s parks and gardens became popular places to spend leisure time, and many were created in order to offer citizens sanctuary from their hard, industrial work. In 1871 the Act of Parliament establishing bank holidays mandated leisure time for the working classes, and many of their number used these precious days off to stroll freely in public gardens, including Kew.

Gleaming new train tracks were laid from London, and omnibuses clogged the roads out from the city, piled high with eager day-trippers keen for a glimpse of the Gardens, which by the late 1800s were firmly established as a visitor attraction, and were now easy to reach from the capital.

The sudden influx of visitors that Kew invited in the 1800s spawned the publication of the first official guidebook in 1847. Kew's guidebooks are of course written for visitors, in an attempt to enrich their time in the Gardens; without visitors, the guidebooks would not exist. The experience of stepping through the gates into the Gardens is echoed by the opening of a guidebook — to read the guidebook is to walk virtually through Kew's landscape.

**Photograph from the 1930 guidebook showing a view
from the Great Pagoda of the Temperate House.**

Some of Kew's guidebooks address visitors directly: "By the glasshouse door *you* will see ...". The guidebooks provide a straightforward connection between the Gardens and the people who visit them; they give Kew a voice and a means of communicating with those who experience the landscape.

Who visits Kew?

For as long as Kew has entertained them, it has also sought to understand who its visitors are, and their motivations for visiting.

Every year since 1893 the Kew Guild (a society for Kew staff past and present) has published its *Journal*, an account of significant events in the Gardens, providing an unbroken annual record of Kew's history. In 1944 an essay, *Kew As A Landscape*, was published in the *Journal*, painting an imagined vignette of a visit to Kew:

> Magnolias were in full bloom, the sky its deepest blue, with white, fleecy
> clouds moving gently across. Kew was the Kew that we all like to remember,
> the Kew of Youth and Happiness and Colour and Leisure. In front of the

magnolias an exultant chuckling baby was being tucked into his pram by his mother, while a young airman, looking equally triumphant, tucked his camera back in his pocket, saying as he did so, 'That one I took of you two should be good — magnolias, and sky in the background. It ought to be a picture.' This little scene is typical of Kew. Kew is many things, and perhaps the most outstanding of all is that it has become a Treasury of Happy Moments for Londoners, and for thousands of visitors from all parts of the globe.

The author is right: many people who have visited Kew take with them happy recollections of the landscape, a place where they have walked amongst leafy trees and admired blazing flowerbeds. They may have visited several times or made the pilgrimage only once. They visit for inspiration and to borrow the very best ideas in decorative horticulture for their own gardens; they visit to feel the history of the landscape beneath their feet; they visit to be a part of this famous place for just an afternoon. Whatever their motivations, for centuries visitors to Kew have carried away with them fond memories of the Gardens and their time spent there.

In his 1847 report, Kew's first Director William Hooker described visitors' motivations as "health, pleasure and instruction".

Kew's second Director, Joseph Hooker, was much grumpier than his father and never keen on opening Kew to the general public. He viewed visitors with suspicion, claiming the Gardens would be choked by "swarms of nursery maids and children who inhabit the innumerable villas that have sprung up around Kew and Richmond".

In his annual report for 1871, Hooker junior tried to classify visitors to the Gardens as those seeking information about plants such as botanists and horticulturists (of whom he approved); and others whom he viewed judgementally as "mere pleasure or recreation seekers ... those whose motives are rude romping and games".

He is not the only scholar of Kew to try to understand why visitors might make a trip to the Gardens.

Guidebook writer Robert Hope Moncrieff, author of the unofficial *Kew Gardens*, published in 1908 explains:

One can see spectacled gentlemen peering into the hot-houses and museums, who may be suspected of a studious intent. But by far the majority of holiday visitors come clearly in a true holiday spirit, roaming here and there like butterflies from clump to clump of bloom or greenery, to carry away a general impression of something bearing the same relation to their own familiar back gardens ... There are some who seek out the first and richest flower-beds; others who love the chequered shade of melodious groves, or the avenues of cedar, larch, and cypress at the less cleared end toward Richmond; others will ask for famous old trees like that horse-chestnut whose gouty limbs are railed in near the river-bank ... Open-eyed youngsters hang by the pond with its colony of wild-fowl, on the other side of the Palm House. Family parties stroll through the chambers of the Palace, empty but for a sprinkling of pictures and relics of royalty. Certain visitors, on hot days, one observes to spend much time in and about the refreshment pavilion.

Also in 1908, William Jackson Bean — a Kew 'Lifer' who spent his whole career working for the Gardens — observed in his book *The Royal Botanic Gardens, Kew — Historical and Descriptive*, that for many visitors the landscape provided a refreshing escape from the grey metropolis:

Without regarding it as the home of the richest plant collections in the world, and looking upon it as a public garden merely, it has an air of detachment from the great city whose tentacles are rapidly encircling it, that no public garden or park so near Charing Cross possesses in like degree. In no other such place can one rid one's self so readily of the feeling that London is all around one.

In addition to trying to understand reasons for visiting, over the years Kew has also sought to recognise who its visitors are, and there is much in the historical record which focuses on demographics, with particular attention being paid in some cases to which days of the week attracted certain categories of visitor.

Joseph Hooker identified that Saturdays were preferred by the "professional and upper classes" whereas the "trading classes" attended on Sundays, and "artisans" chose Mondays.

Reminiscing about 1891, his first year working at Kew, William Dallimore — a botanist who spent his career caring for trees in the Arboretum and establishing the Forestry Museum — recalled:

On Bank Holidays many costers visited Kew, the men resplendent in bell-bottom trousers, long jacket and waistcoat, and peaked cap, the whole adorned with quantities of pearl buttons; the women with wide-brimmed hats gay with several brightly coloured ostrich feathers, some of them emulating their husbands or lovers in the use of pearl buttons and apparently bringing up their offspring to favour the same kind of adornment. They visited Kew to enjoy themselves.

Another William, Kew's third Director William Thistleton-Dyer, wrote in 1894 that visitors came mostly from the lower middle classes, stating "the upper classes, with the exception of individuals with horticultural or scientific tastes, take ... but little interest in Kew".

By 1908 visitor demographics had shifted and William Jackson Bean observed, "Kew has one peculiar charm which appeals to and draws all classes alike." As Robert Hope Moncrieff explained in his 1908 unofficial guidebook: "All classes are represented, from disguised millionaires perhaps seeking a hint for their own newly laid-out grounds, to servant girls fondly persuaded that the lilies of the field can show nothing to match the glories of their holiday array."

By the 1900s visitors to Kew came not only from London or elsewhere in Britain, but, as author Nowell Hall observed in the unofficial guidebook,

Aerial view showing the Aquatic Garden and Museum Number Two.

The Romance of Kew — Where Flowers Always Bloom (published in 1950), "like the plants in the gardens, they are drawn from all over the world", and of course this is still very much the case today. Ideologies have shifted, and one hundred and fifty years after Joseph Hooker derided particular types of visitors to Kew, today the Gardens actively pursue those "pleasure or recreation seekers" to whom it promotes itself as a globally important visitor attraction, and all of whom, as was hoped for in the 1944 *Journal* of the Kew Guild, "carry away a memory of endless garden and sky".

A Royal Garden

Although there are records of houses and gardens on the Kew estate before 1759, many of the guidebooks state that Kew was officially founded in that year by Princess Augusta, mother of George III. Whilst the historical jury is still out on Augusta's appearance, her being described in the record as both "a long-necked, long-nosed, long-sighted young woman" and also as "good-looking and gracious", Nowell Hall's 1950 unofficial guidebook focuses instead on her horticultural intentions; the Princess is described as having "'green-fingers' and fertile ideas, which she put to good account at Kew". About Augusta, Hall adds, "It is hard to overestimate the part she played in the creation of Kew. The modern conception of the botanic garden was in her mind. Moreover she made a good start on turning this bright conception into reality".

Indeed, in the two decades before her death, Augusta did much to enhance the Gardens, and made positive changes to the landscape that are still evident today. She spent a fortune on plants, and invited celebrated architect William Chambers to stud the Gardens with intriguing buildings. When he first surveyed the land, he found it boring and bleak. Writing of it *after* he had implemented his interventions he wrote immodestly:

> The Gardens at Kew are not very large. Nor is their situation by any means advantageous; as it is low, and commands no prospects. Originally the ground was one continued dead flat: the soil was in general barren, and without either wood or water. With so many disadvantages it was not easy to produce anything even tolerable in gardening but princely munificence, guided by a director equally skilled in cultivating the earth, and in the politer arts, overcame all difficulties. What was once a Desert is now an Eden.

Augusta died in 1772. Her final years were instrumental in sculpting the land at Kew and changing the shape and feel of the Gardens forever. In her time the Gardens were private, but it was Augusta who ultimately sowed the seeds of today's visitor attraction.

On Augusta's death, her son George III and his wife Charlotte inherited Kew. George was very interested in botany and horticulture and loved Kew. For him it was a place which allowed him to escape the excesses, heat and cronyism of London, which he detested. Kew was George's bucolic, riverside retreat where he spent many summers living simply: according to Nowell Hall's 1950 unofficial guidebook, dining on "boiled mutton and turnips". However, whilst he could escape the court itself, courtiers followed the King upriver to the Gardens, and Kew received its first public visitors.

Queen Charlotte's lady in waiting, Charlotte Papendiek, very helpfully wrote a memoir of her time spent looking after the Queen's wardrobe at Kew in the 1770s. Ernest Law's unofficial guidebook, *Kew Palace Illustrated — A Popular Guide To The Palace And Its Contents With A Catalogue Of The Pictures* (published in 1925) references her account:

> Kew now became quite gay, the public being admitted … on Sundays, and … Thursdays. The Green on those days was covered with carriages, more than £300 often being taken at the bridge on Sundays… Their Majesties were to be seen at the windows speaking to their friends; the Royal children amusing themselves in their own gardens. Parties came up by water too, with bands of music … The whole was a scene of enchantment and delight: Royalty living amongst their subjects, to give pleasure, and to do good.

However it is recorded elsewhere that the King often hid in the Palace on these public days, and very much disliked the appearance of Kew on Mondays, declaring that after Sunday's visiting day the Gardens "seem so dirty".

Following George III's death in 1820, Kew experienced — quite literally — its wilderness years. Bereft of a green-fingered figurehead, the landscape quickly became untended and attained a shabbiness which was far from romantic, but rather unkempt and uncared for. During those years, visitors were treated with as little respect as the landscape itself, and had to knock at a door on Kew Green to be admitted from 1pm every day (except Sundays). Once inside they were escorted by members of staff who eyed them with suspicion. Kew's depressing decline was not arrested for another twenty years.

The Lindley Report

As explained in the 1938 guidebook, one hundred years previously, "throughout the country an opinion existed which soon began to be loudly expressed, that the Gardens should be transformed into a great instructive and scientific institution for the benefit and pleasure of the public."

The government heard this clamour, and commissioned a man called John Lindley — whose name is revered in botanical history — to investigate what had been going on at Kew in the years since George III's death. Lindley visited the Gardens on a bitterly cold February day in 1838, and found the landscape as frosty as the welcome visitors had been receiving, remarking:

> You rang a bell at the side of a wooden gate, which of itself was perfectly emblematic of the secrecy, the unnatural privacy, of the working principle within. You were let in as if by stealth, as if the gate-keepers were ashamed to be seen there. And when you were there, you were dogged by an official as if you were likely to carry off the St Helena willow-tree in your button-hole, or one of the smaller hot-houses in your waistcoat pocket. You entered unwelcome, you rambled about suspected, and you were let out with manifest gladness at your departure.

Once inside, visitors' experience of the Gardens themselves would have been incredibly poor. In order to write his commissioned report, Lindley inspected greenhouses, buildings and plants, and interviewed members of staff. His main criticisms were that the greenhouses were in a derelict state, a lot of the plants were either dead (not helped by the cold weather) or very crowded, and that the quality of labelling expected in a botanical garden of apparent scientific standing was lacking. Lindley's striking recommendation, which changed the course of the Gardens' history forever, was that Kew "should either be at once taken for public purposes, gradually made worthy of the country, and converted into a powerful means of promoting national science, or it should be abandoned".

Luckily, the government chose the former path, and in March 1840 transferred Kew out of royal hands and into those of the Commissioners of

Woods and Forests. Kew's first Director, William Hooker, took up his post on April Fools' Day 1841, and began his lifetime's work, quickly implementing high standards and transforming the Gardens into the beautiful landscape that can be recognised today. Writing in 1847, just six short years after William Hooker's investiture, Lindley observed:

> Look at the state of things in former days ... How gratifying is the contrast now! You go in by one of the most beautiful entrances that have been erected in modern times ... There is no unlocking of a dark door — you walk in freely. Turn to the left, you wander among some of the more secluded scenery of the ... gardens until you reach the hothouses and the adjacent beds. Or walk straight forward along the bold, broad promenade immediately after you enter — visit the conservatory on your right, and at the end of this promenade turn to the left and ramble along the far finer promenade, adorned on either side by flower beds, lawns, and shrubberies, and terminated by the new conservatory [the Palm House], now in course of erection; its terrace and sheet of water; all bounded by the views ... beyond. It is scarcely conceivable that in so short a time the change from the old close, crabbed, cramped, suspicious, dark system could have been so complete.

The Hookers

William Hooker's instatement at Kew is a pivotal moment in the story of the Gardens and consequently of the visitors it has attracted. One of Hooker's early acts as Director was to abolish the rule that visitors had to be accompanied by members of staff, and instead allowed them to wander freely through the landscape, and actually enjoy being there (on Thursday and Sunday afternoons only). Although William Hooker was not known for his positive views towards visitors, this progressive decision was illustrative of his quarter-century at Kew, during which — accidentally or not — he made the Gardens much more visitor-focused.

During his tenure, William Hooker oversaw the construction of the Palm House, Waterlily House and the centre block and octagons of the Temperate House. Museum Number One was built and opened, and the general layout of the landscape was made much more cohesive. These changes added considerably to the public amenity of the Gardens. In just under 25 years, William Hooker transformed Kew's landscape. Consequently, this watershed era marks the beginning of the period of focus of this book. Victorian Kew and 21st-century Kew are not so dissimilar.

In August 1865 William Hooker caught an unseasonal throat infection, died, and was buried in St Anne's Church on Kew Green. His son, Joseph Hooker, became Kew's second Director. He famously despised visitors, and wanted the Gardens' sole purpose to be an elitist scientific institution visited by eminent and serious botanists, and not "a swarm of filthy children and women of the lowest class", as he saw Kew's visiting public.

When Kew Gardens station opened in 1869, visitor numbers to Kew dramatically increased. Joseph Hooker experienced constant pressure from the public to extend opening hours and provide better public facilities in the Gardens.

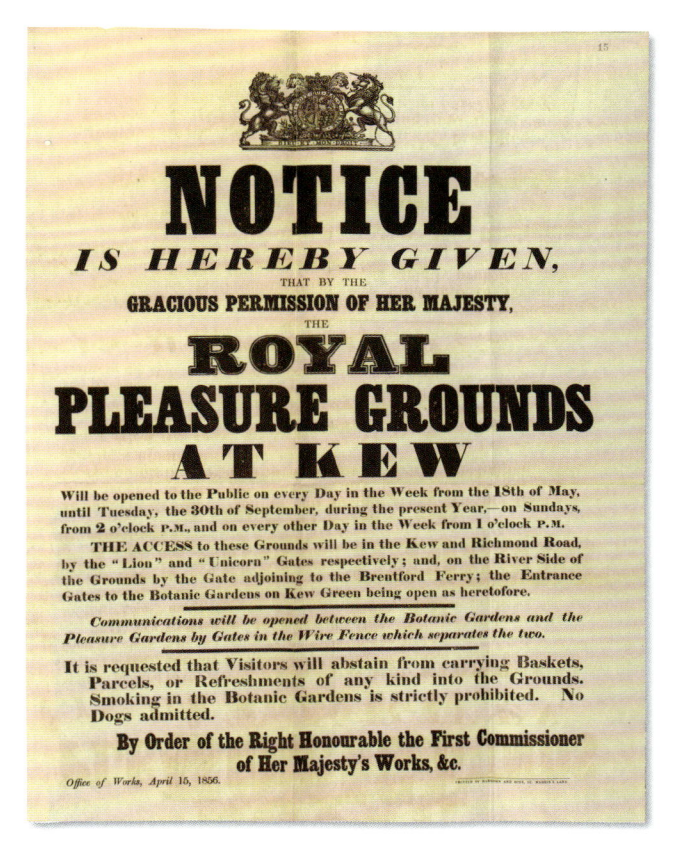

Poster announcing opening times, printed in 1856.

However, as visiting Kew was free at the time, unlike today, visitors were a drain on financial resources; using money which would, in Joseph Hooker's opinion, have been much better spent on funding Kew's scientific mission. Writing in 1878 he explained:

> The tendency to regard the Gardens as a resort for pleasure seekers … has rapidly increased. To meet popular demands larger sums were spent on making flower beds, on the purchase of vases and ornamental work and on building Lodge Gates and conveniences all which have attracted crowds to the Gardens and necessitated a larger outlay on Police Patrols, Gatekeepers and on daily labour devoted to attractions, until now fully three-fourths of the expenditure of the establishment may be put down to other than its primary objects.

In 1877 the Kew Gardens Public Rights Defence Association (described in a Kew Guild *Journal* as "local malcontents") was formed and demanded that Kew be opened to visitors in the mornings as well as afternoons. The Director denied them this opportunity, on the grounds that "if opened the whole day the Gardens will be regarded as a Park. Park-license will insinuate itself and demands for luncheons, picnics and bands of music will follow." However, as a 'compromise' Joseph Hooker permitted the Gardens to be opened at 10am on bank holidays (of which there were only a handful each year).

Following further public pressure, in 1882 Joseph Hooker conceded to an extra hour of afternoon opening, advancing the time posted on the gates from 1pm to 12 noon. This is as far as he would ever negotiate before he retired from his 20 years at Kew's helm in 1885, making room for his son-in-law, William Thiselton-Dyer, Kew's third Director, who obeyed the government's 1898 edict that the Gardens would open during summer months from 10am. This new opening time was made year-round in 1921.

Kew as a visitor attraction

Historical accounts of the public demanding access to Kew show that they clearly thought of the Gardens as 'theirs' — a shared national resource; public rather than private property; a treasured amenity for all. This feeling of ownership demonstrates that Kew is a special place for the many people who visit; a place with which they form a lifelong relationship.

Throughout the 20th century Kew tapped into this sentiment and harnessed it as way of attracting (by then much wanted) visitors through the turnstiles: Kew's growth towards being a visitor-centred attraction rapidly increased.

The 'functions of Kew' are described in the 1912 guidebook; one of which is progressively titled "a place of public resort". The 1951 edition also examines the theme of Kew as a visitor attraction but, unwelcomingly, attaches a strict caveat:

> By a large proportion of those who come to Kew, it is thought of rather as a place of recreation than as a scientific institution, but valuable as the former service is, it must be appreciated as a by-product of the Institution's main purpose, and therefore the usage of the Gardens by the public, must not be allowed to hamper its chief functions as a scientific establishment.

This conflict between Kew's two primary functions, which has existed since the Hookers' time, repeats throughout the years.

The 1990s, however, saw a sea-change in Kew's perception of its visitors, who were no longer a necessary nuisance, but critical to the future health of the Gardens' finances and consequent ability to remain relevant and vital. The landscape was well-tended, labelling became accessible, a programme of events and exhibitions was promoted, and in 1992 the Victoria Gate Visitor Centre was opened to much fanfare. As well as a shop and café, it included interpretation spaces that provided visitors with information about the Gardens, with a special focus on how to enjoy them. This revolution paid off — the results of a 1992 visitor survey revealed that 97 per cent of visitors thought their visit had fulfilled their expectations.

In his 1993 staff lecture, *A Vision for Kew*, Director Ghillean Prance explained that visitors needed to be treated "more as guests than as inconveniences". Interviewed in the Kew Guild *Journal* that same year, Kew's first Marketing Manager, Roger Joiner, referred to Kew as a "visitor attraction", and explained the ways in which Kew was working to improve the experience of visiting the Gardens:

> People come to Kew expecting to enjoy their visit and perhaps to learn about our work; in return we expect them to pay for their visit. Our job is all about making sure that both sides of the transaction end up satisfied. Kew is a unique and wonderful place to visit; the Gardens, the vast range of familiar and exotic plants; spectacular glasshouses; beautiful art in the galleries.

That is the basic product and there is no need to change any of it. It is the things that are peripheral to that, many of them a result of our history, that could be improved to give visitors a better time. For example, information on how best to enjoy a visit; more presentations about Kew's work, improvements to catering and toilet facilities. We must also start looking ahead to more difficult issues. Car parking, for example, can be a nightmare for visitors on a summer weekend … There are a number of short-term things we can do to improve visitors' experience. For example the new map ticket will help people get a better day out at Kew, and it will be supplemented by an insert that will be updated every two months, to tell people what to look out for at that particular time.

In the space of two centuries, Kew's attitude towards its visitors has revolved completely. The defiance displayed by Joseph Hooker (and to some extent his father) have been replaced by a welcoming, visitor-centred approach to horticulture, labelling, access, events and exhibitions, and marketing. Kew strives to foster an ongoing relationship with its visitors, who each year make their pilgrimages to this special place in their millions.

Aerial view taken in 1971, showing the Palm House, Pond and Temperate House.

A SHORT HISTORY
OF GUIDEBOOKS

It is hard to imagine that the idea of a guidebook, in its typical format, is any more ancient than perhaps a couple of centuries. In fact, although the Victorian era was the guidebook's golden age, its origins date back almost two millennia.

A well-travelled Greek geographer called Pausanias who lived in the second century is credited with writing the world's first guidebook. His ten-volume *Guide to Greece* gives accounts of the various regions of his native country, with often lyrical descriptions of particular points of interest — for example, the original shrine of Apollo at Delphi, which he says was knitted from green feather grass, found growing in the mountains.

Pausanias' documentation of his adventures began a trend that has journeyed through centuries. By the end of the 1700s, when George III and his family were living in Kew Palace, guidebooks had become popular, but were known as roadbooks — the word 'guide-book' only appeared in the English language in 1823, when Byron included it in his epic poem *Don Juan*. Roadbooks typically included maps, itineraries, descriptions of famous cities and the curiosities to be found within them, pilgrimage routes, and advice about where to eat and sleep.

By the time Queen Victoria was crowned in 1838, mass tourism reigned. Steam power facilitated longer leisure journeys and cheap printing inspired people to visit the places they read about. On either side of the North Sea, two men took advantage of the business opportunity this presented. In London, and in Germany's Koblenz, John Murray and Karl Baedeker respectively were hastily writing their guidebooks. Both published in the 1830s, Murray's *Handbook for Travellers*, and Baedeker's *Handbuch für Reisende* (Guide for Travellers) can be considered the first modern guidebooks, and multiple editions of these gazetteers focusing on many different destinations were printed.

Aerial view from the 1935 guidebook, showing the Temperate House, Great Pagoda and Refreshment Pavilion.

The two men respected one another; Murray recommended his German counterpart's work to his readers, and Baedeker sold Murray's books in his shop, calling them "the most distinguished guides ever published". However it is Baedeker whose volumes became eponymous with the word 'guidebook'.

Baedeker believed that the best way to see the world was to walk it; in his words: *"sich eine Gegend erwandern"* (get to know a region by hiking through it). In the same spirit, many of the Kew guidebooks recommend walking routes through the Gardens that might appeal to visitors, who indeed have found delight on the paths that criss-cross the landscape.

Useful and beautiful

Baedeker, gazetteer, *vade mecum* — guidebooks have lots of names, but generally only one intended principle: to be a useful, portable handbook which can enhance a visit to a particular place. A dictionary definition would be 'a book of information about a place designed for use by visitors'. Often, they contain maps to facilitate navigation both to and around the place being described, and pictures taken in that place, to provide a flavour of what the visitor might see upon arrival.

In the guidebook, place is not encountered in the haphazard, raggedy, stumbling way it is encountered in life; in the guidebook, place is ordered and systematised. Information is neatly arranged: routes and itineraries are methodical, designed by those who know the place best. Ostensibly, their function is a practical one, but guidebooks are so much more than that.

Souvenir guidebooks — purchased in the very place they portray — allow visitors to take home with them an authentic part of that place. They become portals through which recollections of happy days are summoned; mementos of pilgrimage; proof, almost, that the visit was made. A guidebook's transition from practical manual to sentimental keepsake occurs when the act of visiting comes to an end; in the space of a moment, when it is moved from suitcase to bookshelf, the guidebook shifts from being a much-thumbed and consulted directory to a souvenir scrapbook into which notes have been scribbled and memories pressed.

Guidebooks capture and distil *genus loci* (the spirit of a place), painting it in inky type. They can include beautiful descriptions that highlight distinct characteristics, offering the visitor a printed, panoramic view of unique landscapes, tempting them deeper in.

Old, second-hand guidebooks have most likely already been used in the place they describe, and so carry tiny particles of that place within their foxed, crinkled pages. They provide snapshots of a particular place in a particular moment in time; they are windows through which to see places which no longer exist, which can no longer be visited.

Photograph taken in the early 1900s showing visitors around the Refreshment Pavilion.

The Royal
Botanic Gardens
KEW

SOUVENIR GUIDE

KEW
GUIDEBOOKS

In his 1873 guidebook, *London And Its Environs, Including Excursions To Brighton, The Isle of Wight, Etc — Handbook For Travellers*, Karl Baedeker includes a short reference to Kew: "the Botanic Gardens, with numerous hothouses, where the ferns, orchids, and cacti are particularly interesting". And he is not the only travel writer to have included Kew in their guidebook in the centuries since visitors were permitted within the garden walls — Kew features in a number of London tourist guides and general guides to the River Thames published from the 18th to the 20th centuries. Richard Jefferies, for example, in his classic *Nature Near London* (published in 1883) describes Kew as "a great green book, whose broad pages are illuminated with flowers".

Not content with being mentioned in others' guidebooks, Kew has, of course, for many years published its own. For centuries Kew scientists have attempted to make sense of the world by identifying, naming, labelling and cataloguing. Similarly, Kew gardeners create order in the landscape by clipping, cutting and taming wild and straggly plants to make them neat and attractive. The principle behind Kew's guidebooks is just the same — within their pages the sprawling, patchwork landscape is categorised (trees, water, buildings) and carefully arranged so that the uninitiated visitor can best make sense of it.

Hortus Kewensis

As explained in the 1858 guidebook, attempts to make sense of Kew for visitors began in 1769 with the publication of the first *Hortus Kewensis* (Kew Gardens). Compiled by an apothecary called John Hill, the enormous volume, described as *A Catalogue of the Plants Cultivated in the Garden of H.R.H. the Dowager Princess of Wales at Kew* listed 3,400 species of plants growing in the Gardens (2,712 herbaceous plants, 488 hardy and 200 tender trees and shrubs) and was consulted by visiting botanists. In a way, it can be thought of as Kew's prototype guidebook.

Just over 20 years later, in 1789, another catalogue of Kew's plants was published by botanist William Aiton. It was confusingly also called *Hortus Kewensis*. Aiton's work, described as *A Catalogue Of The Plants Cultivated In The Royal Botanic Garden at Kew* was much more elaborate than Hill's original, and, as detailed in the 1858 guidebook, gave "an account of several of the foreign plants which had been introduced into the ... Gardens at different times, amounting to 5,600 in number." Aiton's guide was incredibly popular — the whole impression was sold within two years of publication (George III bought 100 copies to give as presents). Later, Kew gardeners were offered a cheaper and more portable version that they could consult as they worked in the Gardens.

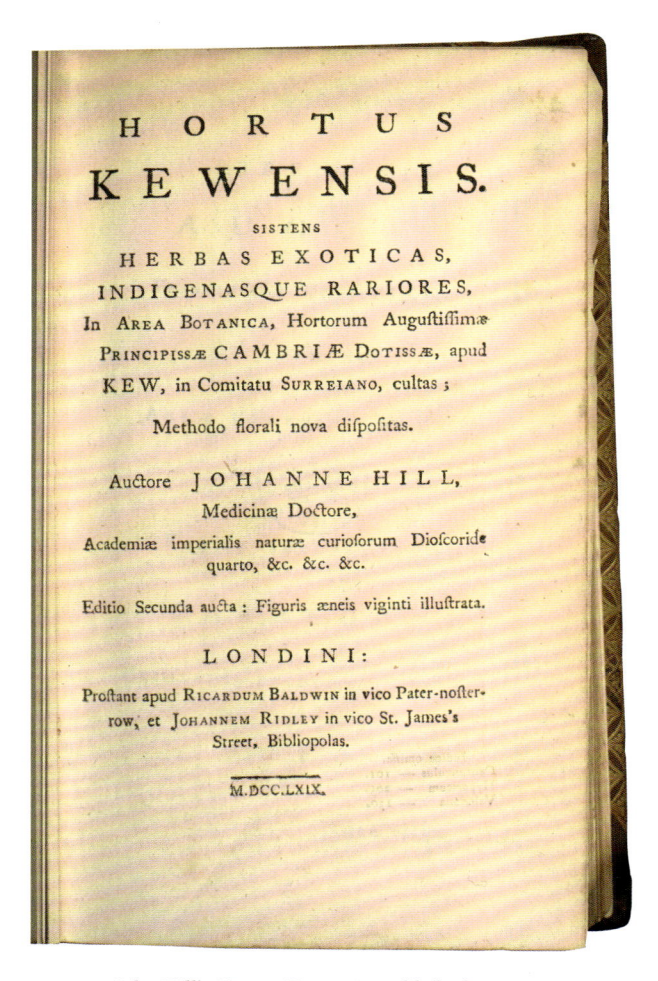

John Hill's *Hortus Kewensis*, published in 1769.

Souvenir guidebooks

The word 'souvenir' comes from French, meaning remembrance or memory. As described in Nowell Hall's 1950 unofficial version, guidebooks "give guidance to those who are visiting the Gardens and serve as a pleasant souvenir". Indeed, visitors to Kew often buy guidebooks not only to enhance their visit whilst in the Gardens, but also, and perhaps more importantly, as a keepsake of their time spent in the landscape. Consequently, Kew's historic souvenir guidebooks (sometimes called 'Illustrated Guidebooks') are often beautiful mementos which celebrate the Gardens through words and pictures.

Once the liberal admission of visitors to the Gardens was permitted in 1841, the need for an official guidebook became ever more pressing. In 1844, Director William Hooker was instructed by the government to prepare such a guidebook. He toiled for three long years, drafting and redrafting, collecting information and arranging the production of woodcuts and maps. Finally, in 1847, Hooker's *Kew Gardens Or, A Popular Guide to the Royal Botanic Gardens of Kew* was ready, and not a moment too soon, for a rival, unofficial guidebook, Jeff's *Handbook to Kew Gardens*, was published in the same year — although it was much less detailed than the official guidebook, of course, its subject was the same.

If Kew was ever worried by this competition, however, it need not have been — Hooker's official guidebook was deemed an excellent innovation by visitors and was much in demand. As explained in the 1858 guidebook:

> The public, having been freely admitted to the Gardens under a few needful regulations ... cannot fail to desire some information respecting them. It is with a view to satisfy such laudable curiosity, and to increase the interest with which the Gardens are visited, that this guide is now compiled.

Indeed, by 1858, Kew had properly understood the need for, and function of, its guidebooks, which, as the edition for that year explains:

> should indicate to strangers the more remarkable features in the Royal Botanic Gardens of Kew, and point out some of the many interesting plants cultivated there, as has long been desideratum. Of late, this want has been peculiarly felt, because of the great extent of the ground, the number of plant-houses, and the amazing increase of the collection.

Within the first 15 years of its initial publication, 21 editions of Hooker's guidebook had been printed. His inclusion of the word "Popular" in the title was clearly foresight.

Not content with publishing its general guidebook to the Gardens, in the 1890s Kew also started printing and selling monograph guidebooks for its Museums, and for the Marianne North Gallery in 1882, the year it was opened. All 2,000 copies of the first edition and 5,000 copies of the second edition of the Gallery guidebook sold within the first year. These guidebooks were more comprehensive affairs, and included very detailed descriptions of each object and painting that the visitor might encounter within the buildings.

As well as the *Popular Guide* to the Gardens, by the 1890s Kew was selling to its visitors a *Key Plan and Index* (priced at twopence), and separate *Official Guides* to the three Museums of Economic Botany and to the Marianne North Gallery (fourpence each), as well as *Hand Lists* on subjects including ferns, alpines, orchids, hardy herbaceous plants and conifers. The *Hand Lists* were extremely popular with visitors, often selling out and frequently having to be reprinted, as recalled in the 1898 Kew Guild *Journal*, "These catalogues of the collections of the plants grown at Kew continue to be in general demand." By 1906 a *Catalogue of Portraits of Botanists exhibited in the Museums at Kew* (fivepence) was also available. Since then, as well as continuing to publish its souvenir guidebook, Kew has also sporadically published other guides on specific subjects, for example Kew Palace and the Princess of Wales Conservatory, and these also feature in this book.

The practical aim of Kew's guidebooks, as explained in the 1858 edition, is to "describe, with all possible brevity, the present condition of the Royal Botanic Gardens, and at the same time indicate the objects most worth the attention of a stranger, both in the open ground and the several plant-houses." But the guidebooks are so much more than this. They are carefully compiled historical records, which reveal changes in the Gardens, changes in descriptive language, changes in how Kew perceives itself and its visitors. Mostly, though, they are beautiful, collectable souvenirs of Kew's landscape and legacy, to be savoured and treasured.

*No more delightful day's pleasure can
be enjoyed in the neighbourhood of the
metropolis, than that which is afforded by
a holiday at Kew; and the time passed in
the Botanic Gardens, amid that wonderful
collection of plants, and trees and flowers,
is as instructive as it is agreeable. For who
does not love to look on the productions of the
earth, and see with delight the floral treasures
which, in all the hues of the rainbow, enamel
the Gardens and fill the air with fragrance?*

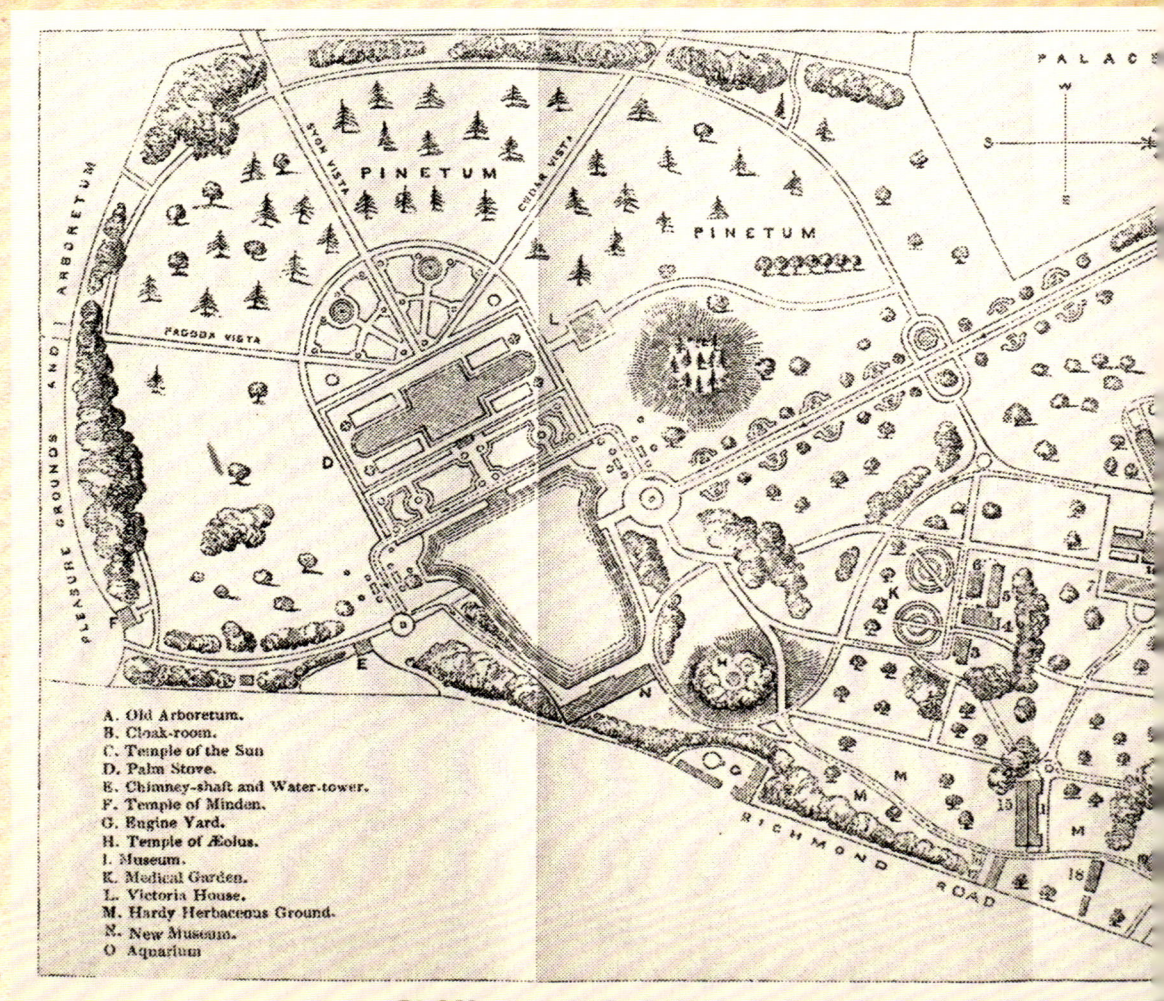

A. Old Arboretum.
B. Cloak-room.
C. Temple of the Sun
D. Palm Stove.
E. Chimney-shaft and Water-tower.
F. Temple of Minden.
G. Engine Yard.
H. Temple of Æolus.
I. Museum.
K. Medical Garden.
L. Victoria House.
M. Hardy Herbaceous Ground.
N. New Museum.
O. Aquarium

PLAN OF THE ROYAL BOTANIC GARDENS OF K

Map from the 1858 guidebook showing the old Arboretum planted close to the Orangery.

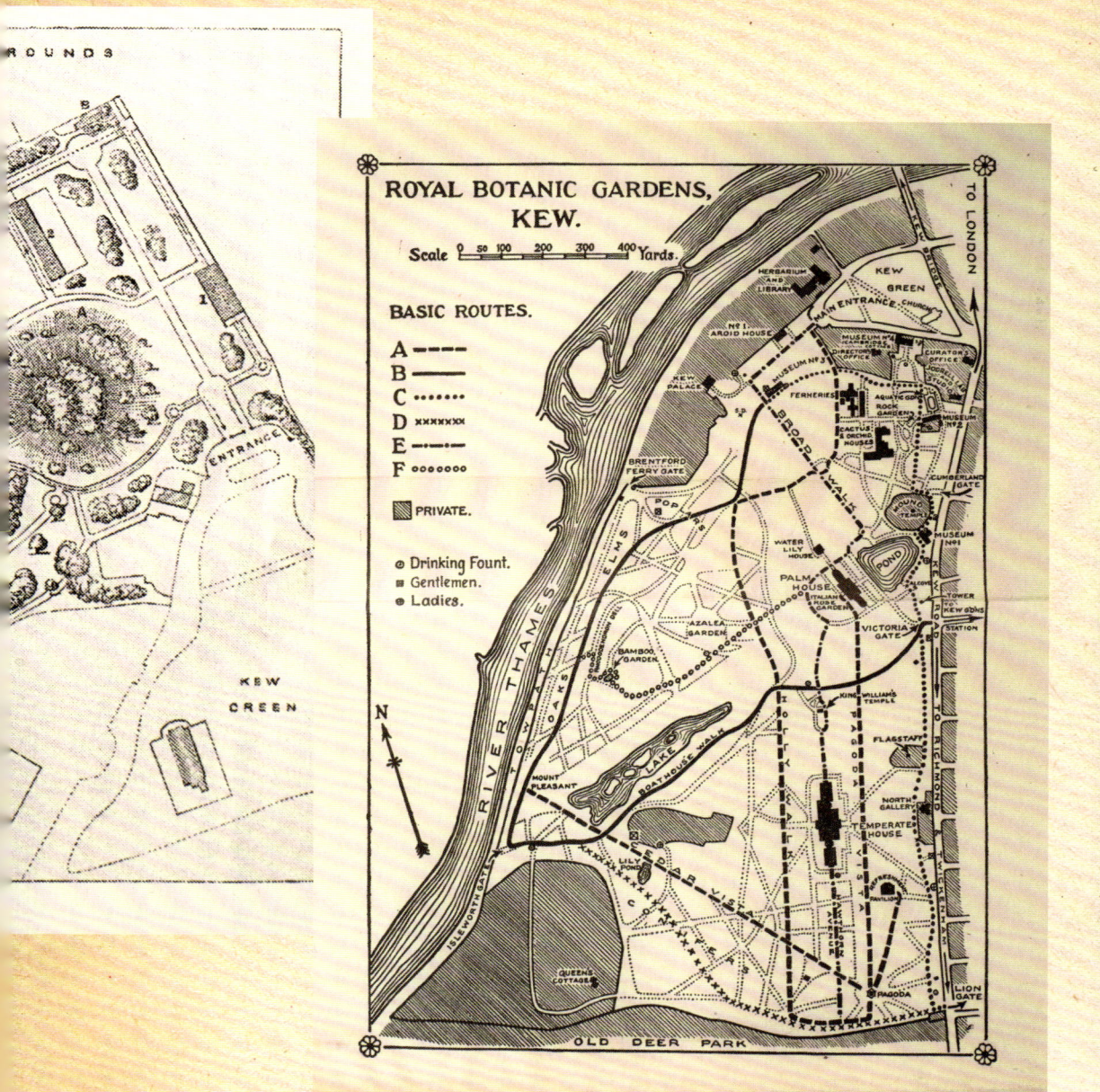

Map from the 1951 guidebook
showing various walking routes
around the Gardens.

1963 fold-out map showing the T-Range and Ferneries.

References; e.g. H17; are to the letters and figures in the borders of the Key plan.

ROYAL BOTANIC GARDENS

KEW

Guides, Picture Postcards and Publications relating to the Royal Botanic Gardens can be purchased at the Bookstall E.16

NOTE: To find any object of interest, look for the name in the index, and opposite to it observe the letter and figure (marked thus for Japanese Gateway I3). Then look down either side of the plan for the black letter and along the top or bottom for the black figure, and the object will be found in the square at the intersection of the lines of squares indicated by the letter and figure.

Scale: Fifteen Inches to One Mile
100 200 300 400 500 600 700 800 900 1000 Feet

Area of Gardens approximately 300 acres
Grid interval 100 Metres

LIST OF THE MORE IMPORTANT SPECIMENS AND COLLECTIONS OF TREES AND SHRUBS
For more detailed information see the Guides and Handlists.

...........E8 & 9, F9, G9	Crab Mound ....G & H13	Hydrangea ....H & J2 & 3
...................J9	Cypress ...F3 & 4, G3 & 4, H2	Indian Bean H8
....E13, F9 to 13, G10 & 11	Daffodil E13	Ivy ....K15 & 16
Border F14	Dawn Redwood...D6, E5, G17	Japanese Cedar ......F3 & 4
.................E10, J3	Deutzia ....H4 & 5	Japanese Cherries H10&11,H14
....C9 & 10, D9 to11, E9 &12	Dogwood ....H & J8 & 9	Jasmine ....F10 & 11
...F6 & 7, F10, G7 & 8	Elder ....D9 & 10	Juniper E6
.....................K9	Elm ......C & D11 & 12, J16	Larch G3
.............D13, E13 & 14	Ephedra E6	Leguminosae ....L4 & 5
....C & D2 & 3,	Escallonia H4	Leyland's Cypress .....E5 & 17
.....G & H6 & 7	Eucryphia G8, H9	Libocedrus ......D6, G & H3
..............H8	Euonymus K8	Lilac ...D & E16, F10,11 & 14,
.............H8	Fir ....E7, F4, F7 & 8	...............H17
..K9 & 10, K14, L8 & 9	Gunnera J13	Lime ....G14, H16, J & K8 & 9
..C12, E12, F3 & 4, F7 & 8	Hawthorn ...J4 & 5, K3 & 4	Lucombe Oak G10
......G & H9	Hazel ....E9 & 10	Magnolia ...E10, E & F11 & 12,
ut (Horse) ...E7, K5 & 6	Helianthemum .....J15 & 16	...............K9 & 10
ut (Sweet)..D&E8&9,F7	Hemlock Spruce F8	Maidenhair Tree E4, G16
e Fir	Hibiscus ....J & K9	Maple ....K6 to 8
..........K9 & 10	Hickory L5	Mulberry H9
...................J & K10	Holly ....G8 & 9, H6 to 8	Oak ....B7 & 8, C7 to10, E11
easter ....J & K5	Honeysuckle ......G & H10	Pear ....J5, K4 to 5
Apple K5	Hornbeam ....E10 & 11	Persimmon H8
		Philadelphus ....H3 & 4, J3

Pine.......B5, C5 & 6, D5 & 6, E5,	Staphylea K8
....F8 & 17, H17	Stone Pine H17
Plane ....C11, E10 & 15, H13, J4	Sweet Gum E10
Poplar ....D & E12 to14	Taxodium...D6 & 7, E5 & 7, J13
Prunus.....H5 & 6, H10 &11, H14,	Thuja ....G & H3
............J5 & 6	Tulip Tree ....F16 & G14
Redwood E7, K4	Turkey Oak ......F16 & G14
Rhamnus L7	Umbrella Pine F4
Rhododendron C8 to11, D11,	Viburnum J8
F4 & 5, F15, G4 & 5, G14 & 15,	Vine ....K & L5 & 6
....H9, H13 & 14	Walnut ......L3 & 5, M3to 5
Rhus ....H3 & 4	Weeping Beech C11, H14
Ribes ....H3 & 4	Weeping Willow H13
Rosaceae (Mixed) J5	Willow ...A1 & 2, B1to4, C6, D7
Rose (Hybrid) ....G11 & 12,	Wistaria ....L4 & 5
...........H11 to13, J11	Witch Hazel ....H8 & 9
Rose (Wild) ...H4 & 5, J3 & 4	Yew ....F4 & 5
Rubus ....J4 & 5, K6	Zelkova F17
Snowdrop ....B & C4	
Sophora ....G15, L4 & 5	Sold at the
Sorbus ....J4 & 5	Royal Botanic Gardens,
Southern Beech ...E9 & 10, G5	Kew.
Spiraea ....K4 & 5	
Spruce ....E6 & 7, F7	

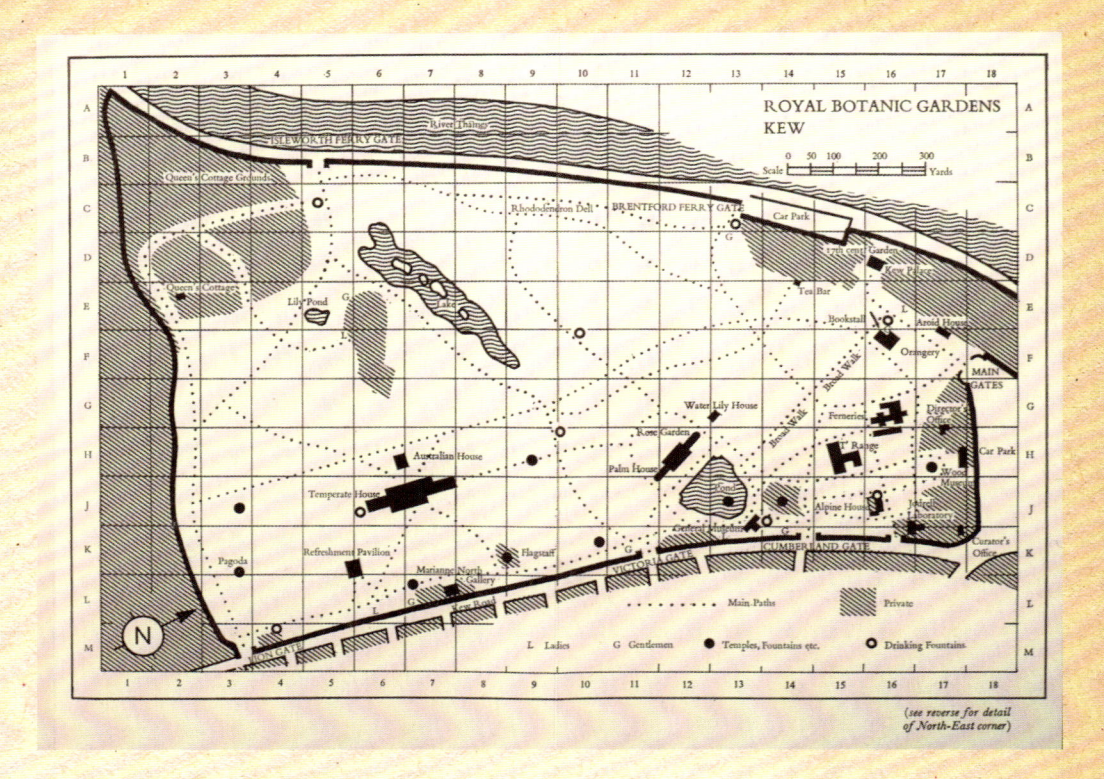

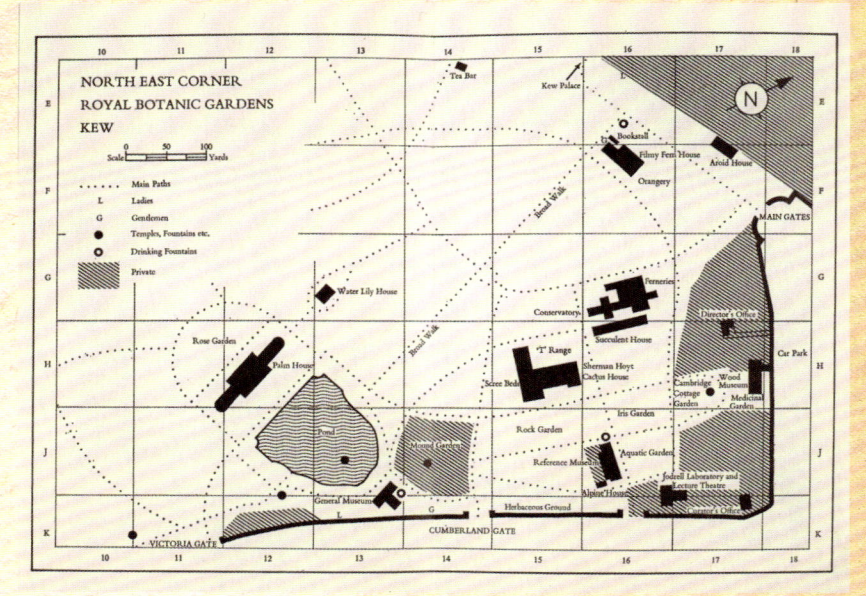

Maps from the 1967 guidebook, with close-up detail of Kew's north-eastern corner.

1930s map showing the cycle shed near Elizabeth Gate.

1898 map describing Cottage Wood as "Her Majesty's Private Grounds".

ILLUSTRATED GUIDE

ROYAL BOTANIC
GARDENS
KEW

PRICE 2s. 6d. NET

BOOK ONE

....

WHAT TO SEE
IN THE GARDENS

EARTH

Trees and plants ... rock gardens and herbaceous beds ... bluebell woods ... and the long sweeping vistas that have the sure stamp of an English country estate

The land at Kew — the soil, the earth — is the oldest part of the landscape. The Gardens grow on the flood plain of the river Thames, and as a result, as explained by Kew botanist William Jackson Bean in his 1908 book, *The Royal Botanic Gardens, Kew — Historical and Descriptive*, "the soil is sandy and poor, and it contains no rock or stone bigger than a goose's egg". Tiny alluvial deposits left behind by the river constitute Kew's literal and metaphorical foundations — in this dirt have lived thousands of plants over hundreds of years.

Kew's soil has been much disturbed and altered. Although at one time, as the same 1908 guidebook details, "the surface of the ground [was] almost perfect level", over the years, dimples have been dug and hummocks created; a great hole was carved out for the Lake, and the land was cleaved apart to make the Rhododendron Dell; a mighty pile grew from the spoil removed to make room for the Princess of Wales Conservatory. The land bears the scars of history, and tells its stories.

Kew Gardens is plural because it was once exactly that: two estates which were, as explained in the 1912 guidebook, "separated from each other by an ancient bridle path, known as Love Lane, which extended from Richmond Green to the old horse-ferry over the Thames at Brentford". These two parcels of land were eventually amalgamated in the reign of George III, for whom Kew was a countryside sanctuary. Love Lane became Holly Walk — a deep green membrane, the Gardens' fontanelle; on a map, a sure, straight line, showing the place where the earth is fused.

Even after the Gardens were unified, the landscape was carved into small portions; the estate comprised a menagerie, physic garden, herbaceous ground, flower garden, pleasure grounds, botanic garden and arboretum — all of which were separated from one another with walls, wire fences, gates and a ha-ha, the last of which was eventually dismantled in 1895, allowing visitors to roam freely.

The land is the part of Kew that has changed the most over the centuries; however, since the final years of the 1800s it has remained broadly as it was then, and time-travelling late-Victorian visitors would recognise the landscape today. Indeed, the only feature included here which no longer remains is the Iris Garden — much celebrated in the guidebooks — over which now grows the Grass Garden.

Kew's landscape features are described variously in the guidebooks as "Special Areas" (mid-1900s) and "Herbaceous and Formal Gardens" (late 1970s); in the 1912 edition, particular attention is drawn to "Interesting Trees On Lawns". Kew

botanist William Turrill, writing in his book *The Royal Botanic Gardens Kew —
Past and Present* (published in 1959), also recognised that "there is so much to
see and study at Kew that even the constant visitor misses many objects of
interest or has time only to glance at some that would repay close attention".
To tackle this problem, many of the guidebooks include maps of the landscape
with suggested walking routes that visitors might wish to follow in order to see
as many as possible of the iconic vistas, flower gardens and special trees.

Many of these routes through Kew's landscape feature seasonal highlights.
Kew can, after all, be enjoyed by the visitor in every season, as described by
William Turrill:

> What one turns to by choice will partly depend on taste, and partly on the
> season. Early in the year ... we can look out for the snowdrops, crocuses and
> daffodils ... Then open the tulips about the Palm House, the bluebells in the
> remote corner marked by Queen's Cottage, the wild hyacinths beneath the
> budding beech trees; and the horse-chestnut flowers strew the way to the
> blooming rhododendron walks; and next comes the turn of the azaleas and
> roses, til the whole area is overspread by ... blooms, in autumn dying with a
> pale sunset of chrysanthemums.

Two incredibly notable features in the Gardens which are mentioned in nearly
all the guidebooks are Kew's Special Trees, and its seemingly endless vistas. A few
of them are honoured here, emblematic tokens of the many more that are part of
the Gardens' history.

ARBORETUM

In the damp grass beneath a sycamore,
a squirrel gathers dead leaves, pressing
them against the fur on her belly.
She scurries up the trunk. From her
home in the canopy, she can see men
working in the yard — gathering their
loppers and ladders, loading them
on to the cart.

The original Arboretum at Kew was not, as it now is, at the bottom of the Gardens, but rather sewn through the land closer to Kew Palace. This explains why some of Kew's oldest trees (the grand maidenhair, twisted black locust and wizened plane) can be found in this area.

The Richmond end of the Gardens has always been densely forested however, and in the 1800s this landscape was carefully cultivated to create the Arboretum that exists today.

The beating heart of the Arboretum, and perhaps the whole Gardens, is the Stable Yard, set deep amongst bottle-green conifers and soaring broadleafs. Once known as the Rick Yard, this complex of outbuildings, shacks and sheds, and a towering, steaming heap of manure and garden clippings is the place where gardeners refuel their tractors, take tea and care for young saplings.

Kew's working horses were also kept here. In the 1920s they were groomed by Boxer Miller, the harmonica-playing pony boy, so called because he liked to spar with everyone he met. Horses were used for many years at Kew to pull loads — the last pair, Zenobia and her friend Blossom, retired in the early 1960s.

In the 19th and 20th centuries, the trees in the Arboretum were beset by a dual challenge: air pollution — coming mostly from the belching factories over the river at Brentford — and the poor, dry, sandy soil of the Thames valley. However, through care and diligent tending 14,000 trees now grow healthily at Kew.

A beautiful piece of woodland

Lovely at all times of year

The leading idea in regard to the botanical arrangement of hardy trees and shrubs is that the members of each genus or group should be brought together on a given area, in order to facilitate comparison and to enable a general estimate of their character.

Oaks, Elms, Ashes … are planted together, usually two or more of a sort, so that they can be found, studied, and compared as easily as possible. The collection now consists of between 4,000 and 5,000 species and varieties.

The lover of nature will find much to enjoy during the summer months sauntering through this woodland. Some fine old spreading beeches are there; oaks, hornbeams, sweet chestnuts, and horse chestnuts. Many parts are carpeted with daffodils and bluebells that give beautiful effects in April and May.

AZALEA GARDEN
AMERICAN GARDEN

Listen carefully for the hollow song of a bell
— a distant tolling, ringing out a memory.
The clapper swings in a bygone breeze,
each chime weaving a thick web of sound
around the hill, making the wood thicker
and darker — a forest haunted by mournful
music, by solitude and loneliness.

Near to where the Azalea Garden now grows, in a place called the Forest Oval, there once stood an old building: stones were heaped together to resemble walls, gilded railings caged them in. Moss sponged over the lintel, and in the turret, a lonely bell swung from a rafter. People called it the Hermitage, but no hermit lived within.

All around the Hermitage, a wood grew thickly, bristly and sharp, prickling up the hill on which the folly stood. No birds flew in or out of the wood; there was no light for them to sing by. A narrow pathway wound round the hill, shrouded by knotted, overgrown bushes on both sides.

The Hermitage, or Grotto, as it was sometimes known, was demolished in the mid to late 1700s, but fragments of it survived into the 1800s. In the following century, another bell tolled in this spot: the Gardens bell, which called staff to work every morning for 70 years, rang from a linden tree. During a ferocious gale one August afternoon in 1946, it crashed from its moorings, clanking onto the turf below.

Today, the Azalea Garden is a much more peaceful place. Previously the American Garden, it was planted in 1882 and is laid out in two concentric circles. The frothy, richly scented azalea flowers appear in May.

*A visit can be paid to
the Azalea Garden*

Azaleas have a special section to themselves

The Azalea Garden at Kew is at its best in late May, providing then the richest feast of colour and fragrance in the Gardens.

Delighting the eye with a gorgeous riot of colour of many shades and scenting the air all around with their delicate perfume.

The Azalea Garden is a mass of flowering shrubs, with yellow, pink, purplish, or white blossoms ... many are sweetly scented.

The azaleas flower in May, and then present a wonderful feast of colour and fragrance. What adds so much to the charm of the scene at Kew is the setting in which it is placed. At that season the young unfolding leaves of the fine beeches, oaks, and lindens surround the garden with a beautiful range in colour from white and yellow through pink, rose, orange, to the richest scarlets and crimsons.

BAMBOO GARDEN

Down by the river, close to the bank where
the current slips by, bamboos grow tall,
straining to catch a view of the opposite
shore. They whisper about the water, and
reach their roots down through the soil,
straw-sucking long, cool drinks, stretching
their stems, bending in the wind that
blows through the valley.

The first bamboo plant arrived at Kew in 1826 — black bamboo, from China, charcoal canes clumping beneath clouds of elegant leaves.

By 1891 Kew was home to 40 different species of bamboo: golden bamboos with slender fronds, bamboos with deep green stems, striped bamboos and feathery bamboos with glossy stalks, bamboos that grew taller every day. It was decided to afford them their own special garden.

That winter, labourers removed several thousand tonnes of gravel and sand from an ancient pit by the riverside, creating a new landscape in which the giant grasses could grow. They have lived there ever since, listening to the sound of the river whispering by, catching its tune in their foliage.

A plantation by the Thames bank

A sunken oval area ... on the east side of the Rhododendron Dell, from which it is reached by a gravel path.

In summer a touch of colour is given to the Bamboo Garden by the numerous foxgloves which are planted in the beds.

Bamboos are valued ... for their distinct character and exceptional grace

In countries in which bamboos are common, it is found that the gregarious flowering of the bamboos is followed by a plague of rats and mice. The reason for this is the enormous quantities of seed produced by the bamboos which leads to a prolific increase in the numbers of rats which feed upon it.

BERBERIS DELL
FLAGSTAFF DELL

As the sun steals behind the trees, the torches
are lit — bright, fiery beacons, smoking in the
twilight. Behind the colonnade: murmurs, and
the soft sound of a fiddle being tuned. The
bow lures notes from the strings and they
rise over the theatre like hot sparks, floating
through the summer evening.

One of Kew's lesser-known landscape features, the Berberis Dell, can be found in a secluded spot halfway between Victoria Gate and the Marianne North Gallery. This charming glade was originally known as Flagstaff Dell, owing to its position close to Flagstaff Mound, a hillock near the Gallery.

Like so many other dimples in the Gardens, the Dell was once a gravel pit. It was created in the six years between 1869 and 1875. Buckets and barrows of small, coarse stones were removed, and the sides were sculpted and shaped to make this sunken garden — Kew's third largest excavation after the Lake and the Rhododendron Dell.

Barberries, which lend their name to the Dell, are tiny bright lanterns, illuminating the slopes in winter, giving the illusion of a thousand glittering lights, sparkling in an amphitheatre. And not too far from this spot was once a real theatre: the Theatre of Augusta, built in the mid-1700s — a place where actors told stories to amuse the royal family, projecting their voices over the Corinthian colonnade and out into the night.

In the 1930s a small, natural pool formed in the belly of the Dell, water lapping over the grass.

Limestone boulders were used to build the Clematis Wall very near to the Dell in 1949 — a home for the big blowsy flowers that sprawled and crawled across it — however, the Wall only lasted for 20 years and had been dismantled by the time the 1970s began.

Berberis is the botanical name for the barberries

A pretty hollow

The Berberis Dell lies due south of the Temple of Bellona near the Flagstaff.

This border slopes southwards and is well protected, but even so these aromatic evergreens from the Mediterranean always suffer badly in hard winters.

COTTAGE WOOD
COTTAGE GROUNDS

Midnight. The river is swollen, brimming with icy water. It flushes against the bank, slapping frost-brittle leaves, soaking grasses with silt, throwing mud and sticks — searching for a way in. At the edge of the wood, where the land is lower, the water finds an opening. Silently, quickly, it slinks between the trees.

The woodland around Queen Charlotte's Cottage was gifted to Kew by Queen Victoria to commemorate her Diamond Jubilee in 1897, with the express proviso that it should be preserved as a special sanctuary for woodland creatures, wild birds, old trees and precious forest flowers.

Kew has respected the Queen's wishes. The woodland is a haven for wildlife — green woodpeckers can be seen burying acorns in the turf, the fallen trunks of oaks, hazel, beech and hawthorn are homes for insects and snails. In winter, snowdrops and the round, buttery cups of aconite push up through the forest floor. Springtime unfurls a carpet of bluebells, chiming in sylvan glades, and when summer comes, butterflies flit in coloured clouds through this wild place.

Badgers live in this part of the Gardens. In 1915, a sett was found under a clump of rhododendrons, its whereabouts given away by a trail of crushed flowers leading to the entrance. Evidence of the badger's presence was further compounded by the discovery of duck and goose feathers, corresponding with recently missing wildfowl.

Gardeners dug through the sandy soil and captured the 27-pound beast cowering in his chamber, which he had furnished with a soft bed of bluebell leaves and flowers. He was taken away in a sack, and driven by taxi to Essex, where he was set free, to roam the east coast.

Cottage Wood saw more drama the following decade when the 1928 Thames Flood — which caused destruction to much of riverside London — found its way into the Gardens at the river bend, sluicing through the trees and swamping the earth.

Snowdrops flower here in February

The most beautiful piece of natural woodland to be found near the heart of London.

Lovely masses of bluebells of such beauty that the grounds have become almost a place of pilgrimage.

There is a thick growth of bramble

KEW GARDENS. BLUE BELLS.

50215

May is the month for bluebells at Kew. Sheets of them carpet the ground beneath the trees in the Queen's Cottage Grounds.

A grassy walk defined by light fencing runs through the most picturesque parts.

Enclosed by a wall, the Cottage Garden feels safe, secret — an intimate space, where, in springtime, plants awaken. A magnolia opens its wide, creamy palms, begging the clouds for water. Soft, warm showers fall on the soil, releasing the scent of roots and beetles.

The Garden planted by the Cottage is just as handsome as the bricks and mortar it surrounds. All the plants feel established, as though their roots have stretched down through the soil for many centuries. The tall purple spires and elegant white blossoms return each year, as sure as sunrise — it is a beautiful place.

It is an old-fashioned garden, filled with lilac, laburnum, Michaelmas daisies and creamy magnolia. In the early 1900s, white and blue flowers tangled in the Blue Border, and a geometric herb garden showcased medicinal plants used through time in healing tinctures, poultices and draughts – rosemary for dyspepsia, monkshood for gout, deadly nightshade to cure scarlet fever.

For visitors in need of soothing their leg muscles, an octagonal summerhouse made of western red cedar was erected in the Cottage Garden in 1933. From there they would have had a good view of the wall, which supported fine thuja trees, clinging to cracks in the mortar and drinking the spray thrown from garden hoses. A branch lopped from one in 1982 revealed 90 concentric rings circling through the timber.

A number of magnolias may be seen

Turning right into Cambridge Cottage Garden ... the visitor will pass under the large specimen of buddleia ... with ... heavily white-felted flowers.

Kept as ... an old-fashioned flower garden for old favourite flowering plants which tend to be ousted from cultivation by modern varieties.

A most attractive walled garden

In one corner of the walled-in garden … is grown a collection of hardy medicinal plants, culinary herbs, etc., such as mint, thyme, marjoram, rosemary, borage, balm, horehound, and sage.

The plants grown here either are or have been used medicinally and many of them are poisonous when taken in the wrong amount.

HEATHER GARDEN
HEATH GARDEN

All afternoon they dig through the earth,
heaving chunks of turf on to the pile,
sculpting the land. Then, the metallic
crunch of a shovel on something hard,
unforgiving. As they wipe away the wet,
wormy soil, the brightest cyan winks
out from the bottom of the trench,
mirroring the blue dome above.

Replacing the Rose Dell, which had grown around the Great Pagoda for
a century, the Heather Garden was planted in 1958. In winter, it was a
lustrously coloured patchwork carpet, an unfurling tapestry of rich pinks and
purples, sprouting over the slightly sloping banks of a shallow valley. Visitors
could wander down the wide grassy path that snaked through the middle,
stopping to admire the tiny tubular flowers, blooming brightly on the coldest
of days.

This part of the Gardens has always been vibrant — before the Heather
Garden, before the Rose Dell, the Alhambra stood here. Built in 1758, this mock-
Moorish building was a showy surprise found in the middle of a wild thicket.
It was supported by brilliant scarlet pillars and topped with patterned tiles.
The room inside was painted with vivid murals. In 1896, gardening staff turned
the soil in this place, unearthing the remnants of the folly. The coloured fragments
they found buried in the ground were as fresh as the day they were painted.

A striking view of the Pagoda, framed in Cedars, can be seen from the Heath Garden.

It has something of interest to show practically the whole year.

Especially worth visiting during the winter

An undulating site to the east of the Pagoda

HERBACEOUS GARDEN
HERBACEOUS GROUND

Every morning, Doctor Stant visits the
vegetable patch, twitchy with anticipation,
eager to see how the dew and sunrise have
swelled his great green beasts. They are
colossal now — huge, veined heads rolling
in the dirt, waiting for their next draught
from the cauldron of chemical elixir.

Careful study of this place, where plants in the same family share a bed, is an excellent way of learning which green thing is related to the next. Here it is easy to understand, for example, how a tomato is the cousin of an aubergine, because they are planted as neighbours.

Indeed, fruits and vegetables have been grown in this part of the Gardens for over 300 years. In the 1700s this land supplied edible produce for the royal family living in Kew Palace, but was also part of a wider network of kitchen gardens across London that provided fresh food for all the royal households — from Kensington Palace to Windsor Castle.

Kew's kitchen garden occupied about 12 acres, and ensured that Britain's monarchy could feast on delicious plants every day of the year. There were peach, grape and pineapple houses, humped asparagus beds, two vineries, two cherry houses and many frames for vegetables. Fruit trees were espaliered against the old garden wall, which still exists today, separating the area from the Rock Garden beyond.

In the 1950s, part of the Garden was managed by Kew's Fruit and Forcing Department, and a scientist named Doctor Stant grew giant cabbages by dosing them with a remarkable acidic stimulant.

Plants are arranged solely according to their natural affinities in formal beds with no pretence at artistic affect.

The leading idea is to render the plants convenient for the student, not necessarily to provide a beautiful array of plants. There are of course a vast number of beautiful plants here, but dull ones are not rejected.

*The whole arrangement recalls the
physic gardens of olden time*

*Many interesting plants, systematically
arranged and legibly labelled*

In this ground are some 7,000 species of wild plants, some set beside the cultivated varieties derived from them. They range from common weeds, coarse field grasses, buttercups, and daisies, to some of the lesser known English and foreign wild flowers. There are, for instance, starry anenomies, clematis, poppies, wild pinks, dandelions, nettles, docks, mustard, cow parsley, the pimpernel, thrift, lady's mantle and love-lies-bleeding.

The woad will be found here as if to remind us that not so long ago our forefathers used it to dye their bodies blue.

IRIS GARDEN

A man saturated with dewy youth hangs
his jacket on the cold hand of his twin.
He feels in his pocket for an embroidered
handkerchief and mops his forehead, staring
into a metal face as fresh as his own —
bronze cheekbones, moulded brow; hollow
eyes watching over the field of bearded iris,
tongues lolling in the heat.

Kew's Iris Garden was originally created in 1884, with the expert advice of iris collector and grower Michael Foster. He was an MP, friend of Charles Darwin, professor of physiology at Cambridge University, and as bearded as some of the specimens he grew as a hobby.

Irises grew incredibly well in this spot. In 1970 there was an outstanding display — flowers held high in the June air atop sturdy stems and sword-shaped leaves.

The sculpture 'Out In The Fields' was cast by Arthur George Atkinson and erected in the Iris Garden in 1929. In the 1950s, a student gardener would regularly hang his jacket from the statue's fingers while he worked. The sculpture can now be found in the Agius Evolution Garden.

Today, the Grass Garden grows in the acre where the irises previously flowered.

THE IRIS GARDEN, KEW GARDENS.

At Kew the iris has an entire garden to itself

Here are collected in a magnificent summer display many of the more beautiful hybrids of iris.

One of the beauty spots of Kew

Each bed is massed with flowers of the same hue and the subtle graduations in colour from bed to bed are a joy to behold, as, indeed, are the veined streaks of the individual flower.

The Iris Garden is formal in design, with beds of bearded irises arranged around a statue "Out In The Fields".

At Kew we may perhaps date summer from the first week of June, coincident with the full glory of the Iris Garden.

Summer dies quickly and autumn arrives,
shaking browned leaves from branches.
Outside the Palm House, gardeners scratch
holes with their fingers, poking bulbs beneath
the black blanket and turning out the light;
thinking of the warmer months when a
thousand yellow tulips will raise their cups
to toast the sweet spring rain.

Parterre is a strange-sounding word. It comes from French, meaning 'on the ground', and this is how the plants growing in these formal gardens are laid out — thousands of frilly, decorative flowers arranged in arresting patterns of colour and shape. One of the reasons for this is that parterres are meant to be viewed from above, and, before the advent of planes, cranes and drones, the only way to look down at parterres was to climb to the top of a grand building.

Indeed, at Kew, the very best view of the Parterres is to be obtained from the balcony of the Palm House. Up there, visitors rub soggy sleeves on the glass, wiping away steamy condensation and peering out through circular peepholes to see the intricate floral designs, where masses of primroses and tulips march with precise, synchronised geometry through the flowerbeds far below.

First included in French gardens in the late 1500s, the design idea for parterres was borrowed from even earlier knot gardens. They travelled to Britain at the beginning of the following century and quickly became popular amongst wealthy landowners.

Kew's Parterres were designed by architect and artist William Andrews Nesfield, a man who enjoyed painting pictures of waterfalls and whose vision also delivered Syon and Pagoda Vistas, which can also both be seen from the Palm House balcony.

Each soily bed originally held one kind of plant, to preserve strict colour patterns, and the flowers were surrounded by 22 large iron urns and corralled within low hedges of box, stone kerbs and white gravel paths. The gravel was soon removed, however, as many visitors and gardening staff found it too hot and arid to the eye in summer, and unpleasantly crunchy to walk on.

Vari-coloured blooms

A broad terrace, with well-kept parterres of flowers beneath, furnished with seats for the accommodation of visitors.

In the great Parterre, or Italian Garden, on the terrace in front of the Palm House … are flowers almost endless in form, size, variety, and colour.

Some interesting and unusual combinations both in colour and species can be found here, contrasting with the conventional schemes often seen in public places.

Colourful and sometimes unusual bedding schemes … are at their best in spring … and summer.

The formal bedding
is magnificent

QUEEN'S GARDEN

Cinders and ash are tipped, still hot, on to
the heap. A volcano smoulders in the autumn
air, brooding sulkily over the view of derelict
allotments and waste ground where parts of a
ruined cold frame lean against rubble from a
forgotten building, and weeds clamber
over rusted metal limbs.

From the top of the Mount in the Queen's Garden, the river can be seen over the garden wall. In the 1600s, before the bank was made taller, high tides would wash this place, soaking the grazing paddock and meadows between the Palace and the flowing water.

The Mount is made from an old ash heap — garden rubbish and fiery rakings from glasshouse boilers, sown over with grass and daisies in the 1960s, when the Queen's Garden was grown.

Down below, clipped hedges echo the plaster patterns of the ceilings inside Kew Palace. The Queen's Garden is filled with old culinary and medicinal herbs used in George III's time: in nosegays, as cures for miasmas and phlegm, to sweeten the monarch's rooms. Lavender and woodruff, hyssop, yarrow, heartsease and sage, rosemary, borage and the yellow sun flowers of St john's wort flourish in the well-tended soil.

The Queen's Garden was officially opened in 1969 by Her Majesty Queen Elizabeth II, in the sixteenth year of her reign. The growing of the Garden was instigated by Prince Philip, Duke of Edinburgh when, on a visit to Kew Palace ten years earlier, he had made not unfair remarks about the unsightliness of the shabby land he could see from the rear windows.

A parterre with a fountain ... a pleached alley ... leading to a mount crowned with a rotunda, and a sunken garden ... surrounded by a raised walk

A replica of a 17th-century garden

The present Queen's Garden is on a site known in the late nineteenth century as the Duke of Cambridge's bulb garden.

It has been possible to incorporate into the parterre, as the central adornment, a very fine Venetian well-head … with a graceful wrought-iron superstructure.

By a stroke of good fortune a small hillock of ashes from the glasshouse furnaces was already present on the site … This hillock was ideal in size and situation for conversion to a mount. It … serves … as a vantage point for the visitor to see both the garden and the house … From it, too, is a view over the river.

On many of the plants there are amusing quotations from early herbals, showing the use to which the plants were put. Various sweet-smelling herbs are grown, as they were extremely important 300 years ago, being used to disguise the flavour of bad meat and to mask the unpleasant smells which abounded both indoors and out.

In the High Wood, a man throws his
mattock into the turf — the blade slices,
cleaving the soil, slitting earthworms.
In this place next to the river the land is
thick with silt; water makes the air humid.
Digging has flushed the man's face to match
his jacket. He plucks at the shiny buttons,
feeling the breeze on his chest.

Like the rest of the Gardens, the land by the river, known as the High Wood, was once completely flat, devoid of pits and dints. In the 1700s George III employed his landscape gardener, a man called Lancelot Brown — better known to the world as 'Capability' — to change that. The visionary looked down through the soil, imagining the beauty of a wooded valley, and quickly put the King's garrison to work to make his idea a reality.

The valley was planted with laurel and called Hollow Walk: a place hollowed out of the flood plain above it.

The soldiers sculpted the land, turning the soil over to look at the sky, tearing chunks of it, heaving sods away in barrows with wheels which squeaked under the weight of the earth. The men were a militia from Staffordshire, and the pathway which crosses the Dell today — Stafford Walk — is named after them.

The Rhododendrons were fetched from the Himalaya in the middle of the 1800s by Kew's second Director, Joseph Hooker. Happier exploring than he was behind a desk, he rode elephants high into the Indian mountains, seeking the seeds that would produce the pink and maroon blooms.

In June 1924 thousands of Londoners made their pilgrimage to Kew to celebrate Rhododendron Sunday, paying devotion in the flower-filled valley.

The Rhododendron Dell is one of the most popular parts of the Gardens

The Dell — it is really a miniature valley — is at its best from mid-May to the first weeks of June, during which period the blaze of colour baffles any attempt to convey its glory in words.

One of the finest assemblages of rhododendron hybrids to be found in this country.

Enthusiasm for these plants ... has increased rather than diminished

Surrounded by fine trees, and planted almost exclusively with the most beautiful genus of hardy evergreens, the winding valley now called the Rhododendron Dell is one of the beauty-spots of Kew ... Even in midwinter, the charming disposition of the ground, the rich greenery of the plants, and the abundant shelter render a walk in this part of Kew very pleasant, for here the keenest north-easter loses much of its sting.

Nothing can be more glorious than the fine show of Rhododendrons, their soft tints ranging from crimson to pink, and from the richest puce through every shade of lilac, to the purest, snowiest white. Their prodigality of blossom — the cloud-like roundness of their forms, fading and melting into each other in the artistic arrangement of their hues, is a lovely sight under the sunshine of a summer's day.

ROCK GARDEN

*Rocks make the water roar — fierce and
fast, it gushes down the falls, frothing white,
splashing into the pool dappled with the shade
cast by overhanging branches. A thousand
droplets become fluid again, mixing with the
weed. Straw-hatted children lean over the edge
to dip their fingers, shrieking at the cold.*

Many different types of stone have been used to create rock gardens at Kew. In 1772 botanist Joseph Banks, scientific advisor to George III, returned to Kew from his maritime expedition to the Isle of Wight, the Hebrides, Orkney and Iceland. From the most northerly of these, he gathered cold, hard fragments of lava, and loaded them into the hull of his ship — ballast for the journey home. These same fragments were used to create a prototype rock garden at Kew.

As part of George III's sons' education, they were instructed in practical skills, including stonemasonry. Under careful tutelage, the little princes constructed in the Gardens a building known as the Stone House. When this was dismantled in 1882 parts of it were used, together with logs and felled tree trunks, to create the Rock Garden — built during that spring and opened in June, in the space between the T-Range glasshouses and the Herbaceous Ground.

Other rocks used to build the Garden include oolite from Bath, great boulders from Yorkshire's Craven Moor and limestone from Somerset's Cheddar Gorge. In the 1940s, sandstone taken from the bombed Houses of Parliament was added.

Around the time that the Rock Garden was being dug, plant collector George Curling Joad — a man with an obsession for alpines — bequeathed his entire assortment of over 2,500 mountain plants to Kew. These were planted

THE ROCK GARDEN , KEW GARDENS.

*The plants come from mountainous regions ...
Their subtle colours give a pleasing show*

throughout the new rocky valley, designed to resemble a Pyrenean gorge, complete with a Dripping Well — a shaded grotto lined with mosses and lush green ferns, where water slowly seeped through cracks in the stones.

In the 1930s, the Rock Garden was enlarged and a waterfall added, cascading beneath a cedar tree into a pool in the valley bottom. Cheddar limestone, it transpired, became incredibly hot under the blaze of summer suns, and was replaced with Sussex sandstone which, being much more porous, retained cooling moisture.

The Rock Garden was very popular with visitors. It had all the different aspects of a mountain — shaded nooks, peat bogs, sun-bleached outcrops, moraine, and when the breeze blew through, it caught within it the sweet scents of thyme and myrtle.

The Rock Garden was originally laid out … as an alpine valley, the main path representing the course of a river, with waterfalls and streams at the sides.

The Rock Garden is at its best in early summer, but the flowering season is prolonged into autumn by the numerous species of Campanula.

In boggy spots in the Rock Garden are placed plants characteristic of damp alpine meadows, such as … the Himalayan primulas.

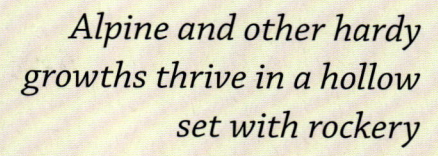

Alpine and other hardy growths thrive in a hollow set with rockery

The Dripping Well Rock Garden's

Kew Gardens.—The Rockery. 70

It may be said that in no branch of horticulture in the open air can so many plants of beauty and high distinction be grown on a small area as in alpine gardening. That is the chief reason of its popularity.

ROSE DELL
SUNKEN ROSE GARDEN

Scotch briar, cock-bramble, eglantine, pasture rose. The flowers listen carefully to the names they are given — by mothers rolling their babies in prams, by the Sunday couple, by the man in the hat who draws them in his sketchbook, printing their monikers in neat capitals beneath their blowsy portraits.

In the 1800s the landscape around the Great Pagoda was badly mistreated. Wide swathes of it were hacked away to create gravelled paths in other parts of the Gardens, and it was also used as a place for burning garden waste and as a rubbish dump for detritus from the Refreshment Pavilion.

Finally, in the winter of 1895, it was saved. Gardeners set about digging a beautiful garden, sunk several feet below ground level and surrounded by trees and shrubs. The following June, the roses bloomed. The Rose Dell was the place to find glorious wild roses: the dog rose and the damask rose with its fine summer fragrance, floppy pink sweet briars that love to grow in English hedgerows, field roses, prickly thorn roses and glorious white roses rambling over tree trunks.

Roses wild and rambling grace
the dell near the Pagoda

Beautiful effects in June and July

A short distance east of the Pagoda is the Rose Dell, a sunken garden devoted to the rambling and wild roses.

Every year a War of the Roses is fought at Kew, a war of beauty vying with beauty.

In the hollow where the roses grow,
the staccato stutter of a sprinkler
sprays a shower across the lawn like
a deck of cards — crimson hearts,
red diamonds, dealt in a clockwise
circle. Droplets fall on petals —
tears run down rouged faces,
staining pink cheeks.

In contrast to the Rose Dell where wild roses could be found, Kew's Rose Garden is a much more formal affair, filled with fancy flowers. Indeed, 170 different species and cultivars of rose live here, and many have splendid names: Ma Perkins and Mrs Potter Palmer are neighbours, nodding their heads across the lawn to Ophelia, Madame Butterfly and Lady Waterloo.

The scoop of land at the back of the Palm House in which the roses are planted is the lowest-lying at Kew, and the plants seem to grow well here. They are fed a rich loam and have an unparalleled view down Syon Vista.

The 54 beds each contain a single variety of rose, and are arranged in colour order, with the deepest reds framed by the white architecture of the Palm House, and the yellow and white roses set against the deep green holly hedge at the Rose Garden's edge.

The Rose Garden was created in 1923. Prior to that, the site was used for the American Garden or American Ground, where peat-loving plants such as rhododendrons, azaleas and camellias were grown from the 1850s.

A lovely combination of colour and scent throughout summer and autumn

To the west of the Palm House ...
is a large formal Rose Garden. The
beds are set in grass and the Garden
is enclosed by a holly hedge.

The holly bushes ... are kept by the
knife to a severely rounded shape,
and increase very slowly in size.

What a show these roses make!
They bloom in stately loveliness.

Each sort is given a bed to itself, so that visitors have an opportunity of clearly appraising its merits

ROSE PERGOLA
ROSE WALK

Frost has licked the ground — stiffening
grasses, hardening the earth. Gardeners kick
the feet of stepladders with their brown
leather boots, securing sturdy triangles
beneath the Pergola. They pick the firm,
ruby hips for warming teas and bright jellies,
trying to avoid the thorns which scratch
sticky red jam from their frozen fingers.

For centuries, Kew has grown boulevards of roses, unfurling petal by petal from perfect, tight buds to glorious full flowers; trailing languidly over timber frames, clinging to brickwork, showering their honey scent as bees tickle their hearts.

The first avenue of roses at Kew was Rose Walk, strutting along the edge of the Herbaceous Ground in 1870. In 1901, a Rose Pergola was constructed beside the Rock Garden.

The Pergola over which roses still spill today was erected in 1959, replacing the previous model. Made from bricks and tile, it bisects the Herbaceous Ground — a floral portal to transport visitors from the Kitchen Garden to the Temple of Aeolus, as they pass beneath climbers and ramblers, admiring blushing pinks and deep crimsons.

In June, as the days grow longer and the nights are warm and still, the roses come alive: showing their beautiful faces, scaling the brickwork, dangling overhead, teasing visitors with their musky fragrance, tempting them further into the tunnel, until they are intoxicated by the heady perfumes and colours.

*A delightful picture
in June and July*

Roses climb over the long pergola

THE ROSE PERGOLA NEAR THE ROCK GARDEN,
KEW GARDENS.

On it is grown a selection of the best varieties of climbing rose.

Given a favourable season it provides a rich feast of colour.

SPECIAL TREES
OLD LIONS

List of Special Trees growing in the Gardens

Many more Special Trees than exist today used to grow at Kew — the historical record is littered with their lumber. The trees that remain — some of which have over 250 rings — are known as Old Lions and are listed here.

Black Locust Tree

Cedar of Lebanon

Chestnut Leaved Oak

Corsican Pine

Japanese Pagoda Tree

Lucombe Oak

Maidenhair Tree

Monkey Puzzle

Plane Tree

Sweet Chestnut

Tulip Tree

Turner's Oak

A low rumble shakes the earth, stirring
animals in their burrows. Noses are
buried under tails — curled balls of fur
and bristly whiskers. The first crack
illuminates the sky, where frisky clouds
gallop and jump. A blazing spear hits
the tree, ripping bark and slashing
claws into its heart.

Kew is home to 12,000 trees, each one of them important for their rarity, unusual foliage, height, age or scientific interest. Some of them, however, are more important than others.

When the Gardens were founded by Princess Augusta (mother of George III) in 1761, she created the original Arboretum close to Kew Palace, so she could admire fine arboreal specimens from the upper windows of her home. This explains why many of Kew's Old Lions — the noblest and most ancient trees — can be found in this part of the landscape.

The original Old Lions include the maidenhair tree and the black locust tree near the Orangery; the frail Japanese pagoda tree, propped on its old-man crutches close by the Ice House; and the vast oriental plane outside the Palace, whose leaves once scratched against the walls of the White House, another royal building that stood on the site. Other grand trees were later added to their number: the stone pine, Corsican pine, monkey puzzle and tulip tree.

The maidenhair tree near the Orangery is a living fossil — its ancestors grew on Earth millions of years ago, and Kew's specimen is elderly too, planted in the early 1760s at the time of the Gardens' inception. At one time it was trained against the wall of Kew's first official glasshouse, the Great Stove, and when the Ferneries existed, it cast its shade over them too. The tree is a male specimen, but in the early 1900s some female twigs obtained from France were grafted on, and it bore fruit — dangling golden autumn baubles that emitted a foul-smelling stench once fallen.

Owing to its peculiar shape, for many years perhaps Kew's most recognisable tree was the stone pine, which grew near to Cambridge Cottage. Its green grenade cones produced edible pine nuts. Before being planted in the Gardens in 1846 it was kept in a pot, which resulted in it growing an unusual number of branches. Over centuries, however, nature

determined to remove them one by one. In January 1926 the tree lost a limb in a snowstorm, and gradually tilted to one side. A prop was used to support it, and in 1955 the pathway beneath the tree had to be realigned to protect the overhanging arm from passing coke lorries delivering fuel to glasshouse boilers. Various other extremities were removed in subsequent years, until finally, in the autumn of 2022, it succumbed to a fungal infection which had devoured its insides and rendered it so structurally unsound that its removal was regrettably unavoidable. Its death is lamented, and it is included in this book both because it is celebrated in so many of the guidebooks and as a tribute to its magnificence.

Tree removal is dramatic, but there is another tree still growing in the Gardens which has suffered several substantial fates. The Corsican pine, planted by Elizabeth Gate in 1814, is Kew's unluckiest tree. It was brought to Kew from France as a six-inch seedling by notoriously cantankerous botanist Richard Anthony Salisbury, and enjoyed over a century of peaceful growth until one day in 1928 when an errant light aircraft crashed into its crown, removing several metres from its height. The tree has also been struck by lightning on more than one occasion — the powerful electrical charges blasting bark from its trunk and scarring it deeply. To avert similar future incidents, the tree now sports its own copper lightning conductor.

CORSICAN PINE

About ninety feet high

Brought from France

After entering the Main Gate, turn to the left and follow the path towards the greenhouses. The first object that will catch the eye is a fine specimen of Corsican pine standing on a narrow strip of grass on the left between a low rail and a background of evergreen shrubs and small trees.

This tree is said to be the oldest Corsican pine in Britain.

MAIDENHAIR TREE

Lacy foliage and fan-shaped leaves, which turn golden in the autumn

A living fossil

This tree ... is a representative of an ancient group of plants, and the fossilised leaves of trees of this genus are found as far back as the Jurassic rocks.

Visitors may notice that the gravel path that passes near the Ginkgo is not surfaced with tar ... in order to allow water and air to reach the root system. We treat our choice old specimens with care and respect!

*Curiously
shaped pine*

Kew Gardens.

*So characteristic
a tree*

A well-known landmark at Kew is the stone pine.

*The seeds are about three-quarters of an inch long and the contents are edible.
This tree is much valued in Italy for the seeds even at the present day, and from
the fact that the husks of the seeds have been found in the refuse heaps of Roman
encampments in this country, it is fairly safe to say that the seeds were sent over from
Italy for the use of the Roman soldiery.*

VISTAS

List of vistas

Old maps of Kew show many different avenues, walks and pathways that no longer exist. Their names tell stories of the trees that were planted on either side of their lengths, and of the people from Kew's history after whom they are named. Some of the vanished vistas are listed here, together with their surviving counterparts.

Acacia Avenue

Boathouse Walk

Broad Walk

Cart Track

Cedar Vista

Cherry Walk

Deodar Avenue

Duchess Walk

Hawthorn Avenue

Hollow Walk

Holly Walk

Hornbeam Avenue

Isleworth Vista

Oak Avenue

Pagoda Vista

Princess Walk

Queen's Ride

Riverside Avenue

Rose Walk

Sheep Walk

Stafford Walk

Stonehouse Walk

Sweet Chestnut Avenue

Syon Vista

Terrace Walk

Thorn Avenue

Tulip Tree Avenue

Victoria Walk

Woodland Walk

Yew Walk

Dusk. Birds roost in dark, evergreen foliage, sheltering from the moon which rises high above the lane, pouring liquid silver into hiding places, uncloaking prowling shadows that slide away towards the river. Silence wraps its shroud around the trees — black velvet, muffling the night.

Some of Kew's most iconic landscape features are its vistas — long walks with terminal focal points that invite visitors to amble down them. Many walks, rides and avenues have crisscrossed the Gardens over the years. The five grandest of these were all created in 30 years, in the middle of the 1800s.

The Broad Walk came first, in 1845, and was designed as a way of directly delivering visitors from Elizabeth Gate — which opened the following year — to the Palm House, then under construction. Soil removed from the land to create the vista was heaped in a small pile behind the Waterlily House and this hummock became known as Crab Mound, owing to the apple trees planted there.

Pagoda Vista was also created in 1845: an atmospheric avenue leading to the curious tower, flanked by dark walls of cypress, juniper, yew and cedar trees.

Arguably Kew's most important promenade, laid out in 1851, is Syon Vista, stretching three-quarters of a mile from the Palm House to the Thames and Syon House on the far bank. Following the Broad Walk model, gardeners piled extraneous soil at the river end of the vista, and Mount Pleasant was formed.

Syon Vista was originally gravelled, although not successfully: the stones were very loose underfoot and were often kicked from the edges of the walk. In an attempt to combat this, they were supplemented with crushed cockle shells, which were brought to the Gardens by barge, and rolled into the surface of the Vista. However, this experiment proved broadly unsuccessful and the grass was reinstated in 1882.

Several dramatic incidents have taken place on Syon Vista. At the end of the 1920s, Flying Officer L. C. Bennett of the No.1 Flying Squadron was piloting his aircraft above the Gardens when he found himself in difficulty and had to

parachute from the plane, which nose-dived, aflame, on to the Vista. The pilot landed near Lion Gate, unharmed, but the wreckage burned for half an hour, scorching the grass. During the Second World War, when bombs fell in the Gardens, an old oak tree just off the Vista was badly damaged by an explosive; and in 1961 a whale was stranded on the Thames foreshore at the Vista's end, where it thrashed about, cutting itself on the shingle.

In 1871, Cedar Vista completed the landscape triangle formed with Pagoda and Syon Vistas. It runs through some magnificent woodland, some of which was planted by Queen Caroline, wife of George II, in the early 1700s. The Waterlily Pond can be found halfway along.

Holly Walk was the last of Kew's grand vistas to be planted — in 1874 — although its route is much older. This is the place where the two great gardens of Richmond Lodge and Kew Palace are woven together, stitched along a seam — a scar where the land was cut open from Richmond Green to the ferry across the river at Brentford, before it was closed by an Act of Parliament in 1785. It was Love Lane, an ancient bridle path bounded by high walls, where footpads and cutpurses made their livings.

A magnificent walk of great width and length, straight as an arrow

The visitor ... can hardly fail to be struck with the beauty of this noble walk, and with the judgement shown ... in the disposition and shape of the beds of shrubs and flowers. Alternating with the large beds are planted two lines of Deodars, designed eventually to form an avenue of this stately and graceful tree.

A charmingly-arranged grand promenade

The Broad Walk … is bordered by beds of rhododendrons, among which are planted different species of lilies, and the smaller beds near the edge of the Walk are occupied by tulips in the spring and are gay with annuals and bedding plants in the summer.

Between the rhododendrons, tulip trees were planted ... These trees are easily recognised by their leaves, which look as if someone had cut the tips off.

On each side ... lie a profusion of beds of incense-breathing flowers, decked in raiment fairer than the attire of princes.

Lined on both sides with Atlantic Cedars

The Cedar Vista runs through magnificent woodland

In the autumn the trees take on the most gorgeous rosy and orange tints.

The formation of vistas has ... given a form and definiteness to certain portions, and has much improved Kew as a picturesque garden.

An ancient bridle path

Long straight Holly Walk, where the collection of hollies is planted

Stretching … half-a-mile … is the Holly Walk, covering almost exactly the track of the Love Lane of olden time. The Tudor sovereigns, when resident at Richmond, must, with their retinues, have passed along this route many times on their way to the Ferry at Brentford, and thence to London.

Holly Walk … roughly marks the boundary between the two gardens that constitute the Royal Botanic Gardens of today.

PAGODA VISTA

Old cedars and scotch pine

The trees are planted at equal distances and in straight lines

On both sides the vista is bordered with different species of trees ... symmetrically arranged and equally spaced, so that every species is duplicated in its opposite number.

Bounded on each side ... by a line of scarlet thorns alternating with spiry evergreens.

SION VISTA
SYON VISTA

In few places so near Charing Cross can so extensive a view be had without the intrusion of bricks and mortar

From the S.W. end of the Sion Vista overlooking the ha-ha, or sunken ditch, which here forms the boundary between the Gardens and the Towing Path, a beautiful view over the Thames is in view on our left. The river here takes a fine curve towards Isleworth.

A level, smoothly mown, grass avenue, 1,000 yards in length

In the latter part of the eighteenth century Sion Vista was a fashionable Sunday evening walk for the privileged beaux and lovely ladies of London ... How the powdered wigs nodded to each other and how the lords and ladies used their quizzing glasses! The nobility sauntered over the grass in effortless grace ... and stars, ribbons and garters glistened on the eye in uninterrupted procession.

WILD GARDEN
MOUND GARDEN
WOODLAND GARDEN

In the middle of the year, the Mound vibrates with summer's hum. Tall grasses are bleached to scratchy straw; crickets sing relentlessly, rattling in dry, matted stubble — about the heat and the blinding day, which pulses and stings. A plane passes overhead, casting, for a moment, sweet shadow.

Cumberland Mound, where the Wild Garden grows, was formed from the silt dredged from the Pond it overlooks. Thousands of ancient, microscopic water creatures permeate the soil, where furry, night-time animals now dig their burrows, creating a network of secret tunnels and chambers deep in the hillside.

The smell of viburnum here in winter is potent — strong, heady vanilla. Witch-hazels open yellow firework fingers, crinkling from their buds on the shortest of days. Hellebores appear, silently, flowers peeping through frost and foliage.

Later, in spring, come the tiny crocuses, early primroses and shivering drifts of pearly snowdrops. Throngs of wild daffodils nod in the warming air. Overhead, elms, sweet chestnuts and a black walnut tree pour pools of shade for ferns and hostas spilling over the banks of a grassy path, flowing through the wood.

Finally, summer returns, and the Mound is covered with golden meadow grass.

There are the Christmas roses or hellebores, whose pure white blossoms are peculiarly suggestive of the season when they appear. Rising out of the brown dead leaves of a year now past, they are the first harbingers of a spring, still distant perhaps, but promising warmth, sunshine, and flowers again.

The real glory of this wild garden is made by the daffodils. It is about the middle of March that the clouds of flower that make this hill so lovely for two months begin to gather.

The slopes are thickly planted with daffodils which for many years past have given a beautiful display

Groups of young people may commonly be seen clustered on this mound, or running, hand in hand, at full speed down its slope

In spring the slopes of the mound are garlanded with snowdrops, daffodils and wild flowers until late June when the bulb leaves have withered and the long grass is cut. On its northern side, under the shade of young oak trees, nursed by birch, there is a collection of woodland herbs set amongst many fine rhododendrons. Most noticeable in season are the hostas, lilies and primulas, but this area holds many other floral delights.

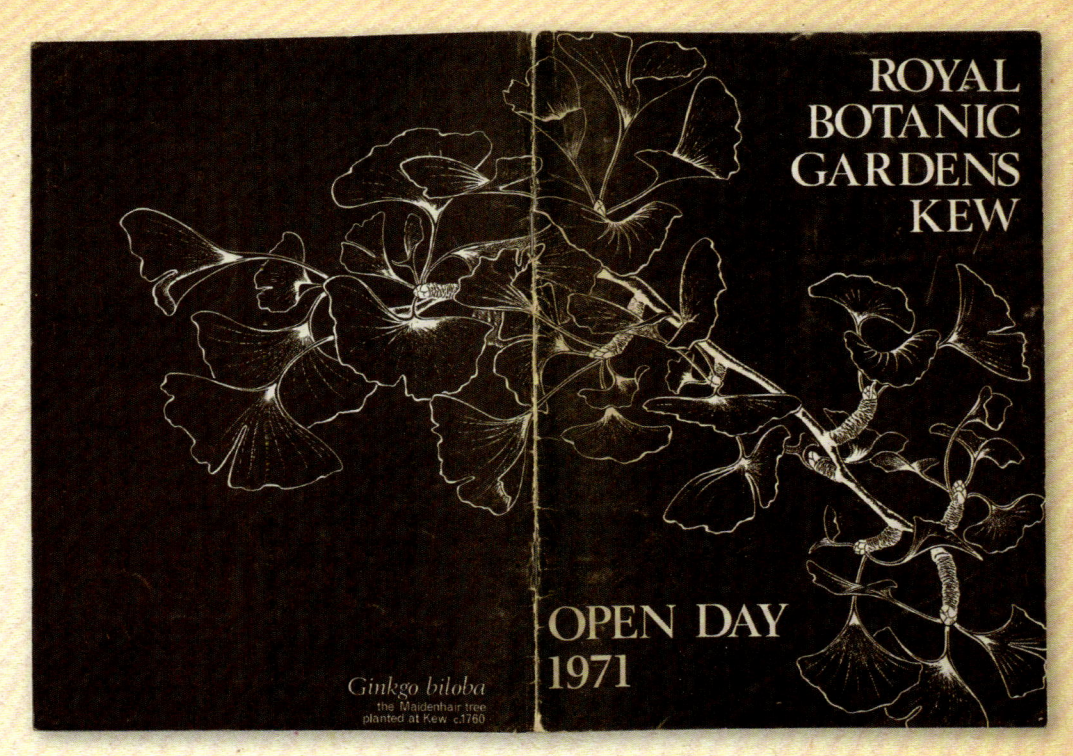

Pamphlet from Open Day in 1971 showing leaves from the maidenhair tree.

Guidebooks from 1930 and 1935. The latter shows a spring scene.

Commemorative pamphlet from 1969 celebrating the opening of the Queen's Garden.

1967 guidebook showing visitors on the Broad Walk in spring.

1970 guidebook showing Syon Vista in autumn.

GLASS

*If it rains, there are
plenty of exciting plants
in our superb glasshouses*

Houses are built from stone, brick and hardwood — sturdy materials that endure storm and time, that afford privacy and shelter. To build a house of glass seems counterintuitive, foolhardy even. But plants and people have different needs, and glass, although fragile, allows plants living in Kew's hothouses to see the sun they need to photosynthesise, whilst offering weather protection for those that cannot withstand cool British temperatures.

Glasshouses became increasingly popular in Britain in the 1700s, as wealthy people sought ways to care for the plants that provided them with delicious outlandish fruits such as pineapples, grapes, lemons, limes and oranges. Indeed, many of the early glasshouses were orangeries, such as the one built at Kew for the royal family, completed in 1761.

In the same year Kew's first official glasshouse, the Great Stove, was built on a site close to the Orangery, now marked by a large wisteria which previously grew against the wall of the building. A guidebook published in 1987 offers a description:

> The first house here was the Great Stove ... Heated by hot air flues in the floor and back wall, the Stove also contained an eighteen-metre-long bed filled with fermenting tree bark in which potted plants were plunged to benefit from the extra heat.

Through the 18th and 19th centuries glasshouse technology advanced, heightening the craze for these structures. Their wonder lay not only in the exotic plants growing within, but was also due to their perceived fragility and architectural innovation, and many people visited Kew to marvel at them. An unofficial guidebook published in 1856, naturalist Philip Gosse's *Wanderings through the Conservatories at Kew*, is devoted to the Gardens' plant houses, which, the author explains, "have assumed an importance almost national".

Victorian times were the golden age for glasshouse building, and many of Kew's original houses were constructed during this period, including the Palm House, which instantly became a visual emblem for the Gardens — and has remained so ever since. Philip Gosse, writing eight years after the iconic glasshouse opened, describes it as having "an appearance of great lightness and beauty". The architects of the Palm House were pioneering, and borrowed construction techniques from shipbuilding, creating a huge, soaring space for tropical plants. The same guidebook describes the novel experience of stepping inside: "a crowd of singular sensations occupies the mind as we are … ushered into the vegetable court". Victorian glasshouses were spectacles of a modern age.

As recalled in the 1885 guidebook, the glass in the Palm House was originally "tinged with green, by the addition of oxide of copper … with a view to obviate the scorching effect of direct sun light, by intercepting a portion of the heat rays". It must have looked like a giant emerald beetle; a shimmering iridescence reflected in the Pond.

This shading effect was also applied to several of Kew's smaller glasshouses, of which there used to be a great number. So many in fact, that when, in the early morning of 3 August 1879, a powerful hailstorm wreaked its violence on the Gardens, over 38,000 panes of glass were broken and the reglazing bill amounted to a budget-shattering £7,000 (more than £600,000 today).

PALM HOUSE - KEW GARDENS

The glasshouses are often numbered in the guidebooks for visitors' ease of finding them on a corresponding map. The first of these — No. 1. — is the Aroid House (now the Nash Conservatory); its origins are described in a 1987 guidebook: "In 1836 the Aroid House, then the Architectural Conservatory, was moved from Buckingham Palace to its present site by the Main Gate, as a gift from William IV ... it was fitted with an advanced under floor heating system."

The largest range of connected glasshouses at Kew (numbered 7 to 14) was the T-Range, so called because it was originally constructed in the shape of a capital letter T. Here could be found special rooms — or, in the 1885 guidebook, "compartments" — devoted to particular species. Those described most interestingly in the guidebooks — the striking orchids, juicy succulents, prickly cacti, gaping pitcher plants and astonishingly large waterlilies — are celebrated here.

Waterlilies are afforded another house of their own at Kew — No. 15, neighbouring the Palm House, a "damp and steamy" place, according to the guidebook published in 1856, containing "perhaps the most charming display of tropical vegetation in Kew", as suggested in a 1930 edition.

Waterlilies are not the only plant in the Gardens to have had several homes over the years — the alpine plants, those tiny saxifrages and beautiful deep blue gentians, have lived under three glass roofs at Kew. The first (No.24) was built in 1887 and is now the Bonsai House. Nearly one hundred years later, the second Alpine House was opened: a fantastical glass pyramid, complete with a moat. Today Kew's mountain plants live in the clam-shaped Davies Alpine House, near to the Princess of Wales Conservatory.

This Conservatory, named not for Diana, who officially opened it, but for Kew's founder, Princess Augusta, replaced the T-Range. A close study of 1980s guidebooks reveals its sudden appearance on the visitor map, and the building was also celebrated in a guidebook all of its own in 1987, its opening year:

This new house, in a single structure, represents a major investment which meets all the particular and diverse environmental needs of the tropical collections. From the outset it has been designed to be economic to run and maintain and because it also merges ... previously separated displays, more exciting arrangements are possible.

The Princess of Wales Conservatory was instantly popular with visitors — almost as popular, indeed, as Kew's original Conservatory (No.4), which featured decorative plants that could easily be grown at home, and was a riot of colour all year round. Nearby were the Ferneries, where visitors could find, according to the 1856 guidebook, "denizens of the dense and humid tropical forests".

Down at the bottom of the Gardens sits Kew's granddad glasshouse, the biggest of them all: the Temperate House. This enormous crystal cathedral is the world's largest surviving Victorian glasshouse. Due to budget constraints, it was built and opened in sections over a forty-year period in the mid- to late-1800s, with the north and south ends (originally the Himalayan and Mexican Houses) added last. In the mid-1900s, the prefabricated Australian House (subsequently the Evolution House and now the Davies Exploration House) was constructed close by — its assembly was recorded in the 1951 guidebook:

Whilst this guide is going to press, and Australian House is being erected on a site close to and west of the Temperate House. This house, which will be 90 feet long and 40 feet broad, with a super-structure of glass and aluminium, is intended to accommodate Australian plants which are accustomed to a drier type of surroundings than those grown in the Temperate House proper.

From the Great Stove to the newest Alpine House, the glasshouses at Kew have protected waxy green leaves (hence greenhouse) and conserved (hence conservatory) glorious floral displays from harsh weather for hundreds of years. Under their roofs can be found plants from the tropics, deserts, mountains and seas: but more than that, their brittle panes, stuck fast in ancient putty, offer modern visitors a translucent window through which they may peer into the past.

List of glasshouses / plant houses / hot houses

For centuries, visitors have marvelled at Kew's plant houses, not only for the green exotics that live inside, but also for the wonder of their pioneering architecture and technology. In many of the guidebooks, to aid the visitor in finding them, the smaller houses — many of which have now been demolished — are each given a number:

No. 1 – Aroid House / Tropical Aroid House / Nash Conservatory / Grecian Conservatory / Architectural Conservatory / Architectural Greenhouse

No. 2 – Tropical Fern House

No. 2A – Filmy Fern House

No. 3 – Temperate Fern House / Cool Fern House

No. 4 – Conservatory / Decorative House / Greenhouse

No. 5 – Succulent House / Aloe House

No. 7 – Cape of Good Hope House / South African House

No. 7A – Sherman Hoyt House

No. 8 – Begonia House

No. 9 – Stove / Tropical Stove

No. 9A – Pitcher Plant House / Insectivorous Plant House / Nepenthes House

No. 10 – Victoria Regia House / Victoria House

No. 10A – Drosera House

Nos. 11 & 12 – Economic Houses

No. 12A – Pelargonium House

Nos. 13A, 13B, 14A & 14B – Orchid Houses

No. 14C – Objects of Special Interest / Special Exhibitions House

No. 15 – Waterlily House / Tropical Aquarium / Tropical Waterlily House

No. 24 – Alpine House

ALPINE HOUSE

In the Alpine House, a tiny violet flower
is growing in a crack in the rock. It comes
from a faraway mountain, where the sun
pours the shadow of the peaks on the lush
green meadows below, and hundreds of
blooms puncture the last of the melting
snow with their frilly fists and faces.

Kew's first Alpine House was built in 1887. It can still be seen in the Gardens today, filled with bonsai trees, standing next to the building that was once Museum Number Two. The glasshouse is long and low, with two gravelled benches suspended on either side of the central pathway. Visitors were encouraged to enter through one door and exit through another, stopping to look at the tiny delicate plants inside as they moved past them like mountain breezes.

Almost one hundred years later, Kew's second Alpine House was opened close to Cambridge Cottage Garden. It was a whimsical building — a huge glass pyramid, floating above a moat which captured the cool water flooding down the window panes when it rained.

Inside, dry gusts swirled through the louvered roof, breathing over the sweet flowers growing inside — campanula bells, frilly pink dianthus, green cushions of saxifrage, starry gold sedum, pretty primulas.

The second house was dismantled in 2004 to make room for an extension to the nearby Jodrell Laboratory, giving the scientists more space.

Today, the Davies Alpine House, with its double rainbow arcs, stands next to the Princess of Wales Conservatory.

One hundred species of beautiful flowering plants

No department of gardening is more fascinating, and ... more popular, than the cultivation of Alpine and rock plants.

The advantage of this house is that the blossoms are seen here in far greater perfection than in the open as they do not suffer from the inclement conditions of the weather.

Protection from the rigours
of an English spring

It is really an appendage of the Rock Garden and is devoted to the display, chiefly from December to May, of early flowering alpine plants in pots, mostly of too delicate a nature or perhaps too costly or too rare to be trusted out-of-doors entirely.

Dwarf cyclamens, snowdrops, and the early flowering crocuses, dwarf irises, scillas, saxifrages, star-of-Bethlehem, etc.

SECOND ALPINE HOUSE

Exceptionally well ventilated

Three thousand different montane plants

The house is pyramid-shaped reflecting a mountain form. There are no gutters and the rainwater runs directly into a moat which … provides an architectural feature whereby the house 'floats'.

Spring is the best season for this house with its miniature iris and cyclamen, primulas and saxifrages, tulips and a myriad other blossoms.

> Here is the Conservatory, cast in the shape of an ancient temple, borrowed from a city where dust and heat rise in the pink dawn light, as the first trams rattle past the ruins and souvenir sellers drink thick, black coffee, staking their pitches for the day.

Named for its legendary architect John Nash, who designed Buckingham Palace, this Conservatory was transported from the grounds of that royal residence to Kew in 1836.

Designed to resemble a Greek temple and originally one of four pavilions Nash had conjured to complement the Palace, it was moved stone by stone on the orders of William IV, son of George III, after it was deemed to have been built in too shady a spot in Buckingham Palace gardens.

Once at Kew, the building at first housed monkey puzzle and eucalyptus trees; then, in 1861, the building became the Aroid House (No.1), the oldest of Kew's 19th-century glasshouses.

Aroids are known for their large, leathery leaves, and are often popular houseplants, such as the Swiss cheese plant. A wild British species is the deadly-looking lords-and-ladies.

The temperature of the Conservatory was kept at 32 degrees Celsius and the humidity made the tropical environment steamy and moist. As well as aroids, ginger and bananas also grew in the building.

In 1974 the outside of the glasshouse was given a jolly good scrub, revealing its handsome cream exterior. At the end of that decade, it was used as a place to store palms whilst the Palm House underwent major restoration.

By far the oldest planthouse in the Gardens

We find ourselves before a classical building having little of the external characters of a conservatory, and indeed frequently on this account called the Architectural Greenhouse.

The Aroid House ... is close packed with a ... congregation of swollen greenery, sucking in the edifying moisture that congeals on the glassy walls, and blinds for a minute or two one's spectacled eyes, suddenly brought from the atmosphere of our zone to that of the equator.

The aroids, including ginger and arrowroot, grow mainly in hot, moist tropical forests, although lords-and-ladies of the English hedgerows are of the same family.

*Some of the species have …
rather leathery leaves*

The visitor will be impressed by the climbing species … that ascend the walls and wind up the pillars.

AUSTRALIAN HOUSE

Jock Slater's hands are a map of the land: dirty creases contour his sun-weathered skin. In his roughened palm he holds a delicate basket, laced with fine grasses and lined with soft green moss — pungent with the warm, oily smell of feathers, decorated with tiny seeds.

In winter, when Kew's frosted landscape was powder-white and evergreen, bright yellow wattle was in full bloom in the Australian House — sunshine pompoms starkly bright against the low, grey days outside.

When this prefabricated glasshouse opened in 1952, it was the largest at Kew, save for the Palm House and Temperate House, the latter of which it squatted behind. Some of the Australian plants that had previously lived in the Temperate House were wheeled and winched into this new aluminium hangar.

Ten years later, in 1962, whilst he was pruning the sweet-smelling vegetation growing near the roof, a gardener named Jock Slater discovered a sparrow's nest high up in the rafters.

In 1995 the glasshouse became the Evolution House, complete with fake dinosaur footprints heavily stamped into the concrete floor. After several years, the building then stood empty, almost derelict, before being brought back from near-extinction as the Davies Exploration House in 2018.

Plants and shrubs from hot and dry regions

Very colourful is the bottle brush with its scarlet stamens

The House is intended primarily for the culture of plants from the low rainfall and more arid areas of Australia.

Plants such as the eucalyptus … kangaroo paw and Sturt's desert pea may seem strange.

Visitors crowd under the glazed roof,
vibrating like bluebottles trapped behind a
window. They pull notebooks from pockets
and cameras from bags, scrawling thoughts
across curled pages, smearing memories on
film. At home, on windowsills and in stifling
greenhouses, they grow their own — gaudy
reds and yellows, wrestling for attention.

The smell inside House No.4, the Conservatory, was delicious — like a florist's shop on a Saturday morning, like a church after a wedding; heady, rich, forever summer — that honeyed, nectary fragrance mixed with loam and heat.

Here, all year round, were showy, colourful plants, chosen for their spectacular flowers and attractive foliage: cyclamen, sweet honeysuckle, hydrangeas, bright daffodils, dangling fuchsias, hyacinths, gardenias and scarlet begonias, blooming for the fervent throngs of visitors who streamed through the doors of this most popular glasshouse come rain or shine. Even in wintry weather, when Kew's outdoor landscape was mostly grey and bare, the gardening staff ensured the Conservatory was decorated with floral cheer.

Here, visitors liked to see plants that they could easily grow in their own gardens, taking inspiration back to their terraced plots and window boxes.

Having enjoyed many years of popularity, the cruciform glasshouse, part of the T-Range, was eventually dismantled in 1983 in favour of the modern Princess of Wales Conservatory.

Filled throughout the year with showy flowering plants

It is the most popular house in Kew. On Sundays in March and April, which are the months when the house is most brilliant in its display, its paths are ... thronged, and there is frequently a crowd at the entrances not unlike that at the pit door of a theatre.

A riot of colour

Much judgement and foresight are needed to keep this large house gay the year through.

Bulbs in spring … fuchsias in summer, followed by begonias in the autumn with chrysanthemums and azaleas in the winter.

This Conservatory is very remarkable for the exquisite beauty and variety of foliage, and the gorgeous splendour, artistic combination and skilful contrast of colour of the various and costly plants, which here blossom — garlanding, festooning and adorning the crystal walls, roof, and centre of this most beautiful and unique "Temple of Flora".

FERNERIES

The ferns are old. Older than the glasshouse, older than the land underneath. They cling tightly to history, gripping on to fissures in time, scattering spores through remote geology. They press themselves into the fossil record, leaving behind ghostly traces of fronds, of damp leaves and spongy curls.

The Great Stove, Kew's very first proper glasshouse, once stood across the path from the place the Ferneries would eventually be constructed. Alas, after 100 years, the Stove became ruinous, and was finally pulled down in 1861.

A little over 30 years later, the Ferneries were built close by, near to where the Princess of Wales Conservatory now stands. Three separate rooms provided different growing environments for delicate, ancient ferns, and their frondy friends: the clubmosses and horsetails.

The bay to the south of the Tropical Fern House was known by gardeners as 'The Chapel' as it felt like a sacred space. Green glass was used in the windows and when the sun shone, verdant, dappled light rippled over lacy leaves, summoning a stillness and quiet.

The flimsiest of all the ferns are the filmy varieties. Their skin is only one cell thick, and their house eventually had to be closed to visitors, whose constant passage through the open door resulted in the plants shrivelling and dying.

In 1965 a new 'double skin' Filmy Fern House was constructed at the rear of the Orangery, where the ferns could grow peacefully behind glass in their humid and shady indoor forest.

Gracefully curving leaves ... elegant tracery

Many beautiful ferns

Devoted to ferns from moist, tropical forests.

The hot and humid atmosphere is that of a tropical rainforest or jungle, the natural home of most plants here.

Containing a varied and interesting collection of tropical and tree ferns, and nothing can exceed the varied beauty and elegance of their leaves, or fronds.

*The arching foliage …
is particularly beautiful*

*We find ourselves still
in the midst of ferns*

In the Filmy Fern House are collected the various ferns which require conditions of shade and great moisture owing to the delicacy of their fronds.

The plants grow in the dim light characteristic of the interior of an evergreen forest. The fronds of these ferns are very thin and delicate, almost transparent.

Owing to the difficulties of maintaining these filmy ferns in cultivation, this house is not usually open to the public, but any bona fide student may obtain special permission from the Director to see the collection.

TEMPERATE FERN HOUSE
COOL FERN HOUSE (NO.3)

Ferns which ... are not hardy
in the British Isles

A choice collection of such ferns as do not require the tropical heat of house No.2.

Here is cultivated a class of plants ... requiring a cooler temperature.

Ferns and fern allies which are inhabitants of the cooler regions of the globe.

Green fronds

PALM HOUSE
PALM STOVE

On the balcony, the iron has corroded
— rust scratches its fingers over the
paintwork, picking scabs which flake
and fall. Below, a forest fire is burning.
Smoke clings in the air — a sodden grey
blanket moving above the shining floor,
where dying insects writhe and scrape.

Victorian Britons were obsessed with palms. There were palms in the parlour, palms fronding against the patterned wallpaper of the drawing room — palms pervaded palaces and tenements across the land. Part of the reason for this national passion began at Kew.

The Palm House took four years to build, and was opened in November 1848. When visitors entered for the first time, they stepped into a new, green world. A cloud of steamy heat enveloped them, the moisture catching in their lungs and beading on their woollen coats.

Thousands of strange shrubs and trees bearing bunches of bright tropical fruit surrounded them: winding vines with coloured floral trumpets twined upwards, wrapping themselves around the cast iron sunflowers and scrolls decorating the spiral stairs. Up on the balcony, visitors looked down through shafts of sunlight into the dense, wet forest, imagining they were wild parrots perched high in the canopy. For Victorian visitors, the Palm House was an extraordinary, green-glowing dreamy wonder, the like of which they had never experienced before.

During its earliest years, the Palm House was an elemental place, of fire and of water. One of the most unpopular gardening jobs at Kew was to unload coal from barges moored on the river and cart it back to the Gardens. These black lumps were used to fuel the furnaces burning brightly day and night beneath the Palm House. The resulting warm air rose through ornate iron gratings in the floor, maintaining a perpetual summer.

Flames were also later used to control Palm House pests such as mealybug, red spiders, aphids and whitefly — contraband tobacco seized at the border by HM Customs and Revenue was set alight in special braziers, and as the smoke wafted through the House hundreds of stunned bugs fell to the ground.

Despite multiple warnings from gardening staff about the swampy nature of the landscape, the glasshouse was built on the lowest-lying, boggiest part of Kew, and underground streams flooded the Palm House basement on several occasions, sizzling out the stokehole fires. Pumps were used to flush the subterranean tunnels, the walls of which were subsequently waterproofed.

In the 1990s a watery reflection of earlier floods was opened in the Palm House basement: a marine display, where coral, flickering fish, red weeds and seahorses bobbed about in illuminated tanks.

The Palm House has been restored on several occasions during its lifetime. The most extensive restoration was undertaken in the 1980s, when the glasshouse was gutted of all but one of its plants and the bony bare ribs of the building could be seen for the first time since its construction.

Most of the plants were moved, using rollers and sweat, to the Temporary Palm House near Kew Palace; their journey across the Gardens was the first time they had ever been outside. But one of their number remained, watching over the renovation of its home like a frail old man — a giant South African cycad. It is the oldest pot plant in the world, having arrived at Kew on a wooden sailing ship in 1775. It weighs over a tonne and is propped up on metal crutches.

The Palm House was officially reopened in November 1990 by Her Majesty Queen Elizabeth the Queen Mother, nearly 150 years since visitors first crossed the threshold of this glass palace of palms.

The large structure of glass and iron, known as the Palm House, is situated close to the Victoria Gate and will be noticed at once on entering.

The Palm House at Kew, even now, is one of the very finest plant-houses in the world. Its graceful lines and admirable proportions make it as pleasing to the eye as it is possible for a structure of iron and glass to be.

The glory of the Gardens

We catch sight of that noble stove, which is perhaps the most magnificent structure of its kind in the world — the Palm-stove. Truly this is a magnificent work, worthy of this great nation, and of the delightful science the interests of which it is so eminently calculated to advance.

Chiefly occupied by large palms

This huge hot-house enshrines a medley collection of tropical forms, grand and graceful.

Princes of vegetation, the royal tribe of palms

Enter the Palm House and you might well be in a remote green world thousands of miles from London. It is a miniature jungle, reduced to order and robbed of danger. The fiercest form of animal life to be found in it are the sparrows and the other little birds who flutter about under the roof and chirrup all day long. Against the prevailing green, a luminous, sunny green, are splashed the brilliant colours of tropical flowers. Here thousands of trees, ferns and other plants grow in orderly confusion, all reaching upward to the sunlight. The air is heavy with warm scents. There is the all-pervading drip-drip of water, for the inhabitants of the palm house are always thirsty. It is so peaceful that the visitor is tempted to speak in whispers.

A great variety of tropical trees and shrubs

We will walk round the gallery and take a bird's-eye view … from the vantage-ground of that elevation. Let us mount the northern steps, this spiral staircase of iron, which by its lightness and elegance is worthy of a place among these charming forms of vegetation. As we wind round and round, up and up, higher and higher, two or three noble plants close to the stairs start from the mass of inferior foliage below, and accompany our course to the top.

We shall be delighted with the multitude of graceful climbing plants that trail all along the whole extent of the rails, entwine around the staircases, wind up the supporting pillars, and hang down here and there in pendent strings or luxuriant festoons and chaplets almost to the floor below.

What strange and useful things grow in the Palm House!

We must now direct attention to some of the numerous objects in the Palm-house, a structure especially intended for the cultivation of those "Princes" of the vegetable kingdom, but by no means confined to them.

Owing to the wealth of material in this house only a few of the more interesting plants can be mentioned in a short guide.

The Bamboo, when fully grown, is infinitely more gigantic than its ally the sugar cane.

Interior, Palm House, Kew Gardens

INTERIOR OF PALM-HOUSE.

Plants in this house are in remarkably vigorous health

Young and eupeptic visitors will inquire for the coco-nut, whose fruit reaches them only in a dry, curdled, shrunken state, poorly representing its fibrous green globes filled with soft butter and refreshing milk.

The paw-paw … has a fruit with a most delicate flavour, when eaten with lemon. A luscious cool drink can be made from it.

The bananas ripen perfectly in great bunches among the ragged green fronds.

PRINCESS OF WALES CONSERVATORY

The Princess wears an emerald dress
fastened with a snow-white sash; her heels
click on the newly laid flagstones. The green
coins of a money plant spill playfully onto
a pathway, tickling her ankles. She shakes
hands with a girl wearing freckles, who
presents a crinkly cellophane bouquet.

Deep beneath the wet, succulent fronds and dry aloe beds, beneath the screens and switches in the throbbing electrical room, the earth on which the Princess of Wales Conservatory is built hides a secret — this is the site of Kew's 18th-century botanical garden, grown for Princess Augusta, mother of George III. The glasshouse is named for her.

In July 1987 the building was opened by one of Augusta's successors to the role — Diana, Princess of Wales. When she died ten years later, Kew gardeners fashioned a wreath of lily flowers and placed it in the building. Visitors came to see it, leaving their own floral tributes and writing their condolences in a special book.

When they were first conceived in the mid-1970s, the designs for the Conservatory were pioneering — the glasshouse would be a technologically advanced masterpiece of futuristic design. And so it was. Replacing the patchwork T-Range complex, which was suffering badly from wood rot, the Conservatory is a single structure made from hardwearing steel and aluminium.

From cool deserts to steaming hot rainforests, the Conservatory has ten different climatic zones, all powered by a central computer that commands misters to spray, vents in the roof to open, and the boilers to pump out more heat.

The revolutionary technology clearly benefits the plants growing inside — in the 1990s two enormous specimens bloomed: a giant waterlily achieved recognition in the *Guinness Book of Records* with a leaf measuring over eight feet in diameter; the following year the corpse flower opened, and visitors queued round the building to marvel at its size and catch a whiff of its fishy, rubbery stench.

Borrowing an idea from Kew's first official glasshouse, the Great Stove, where pots were plunged into fermenting bark chips to keep plants warm, much of the Conservatory is sunk below ground level to capture heat from the earth packed around it. The soil removed to make room for the building was heaped on a mountainous pile on which the Hive now crouches.

At noon on 22 March 1985, when the foundations of the Conservatory were laid, Sir David Attenborough placed within them a spherical fish bowl of a time capsule, stuffed with seeds and books. It rests under the cacti, and will be opened in 2085.

Diamond-shaped

The stunning Princess of Wales Conservatory … holds plants ranging from tiny orchids to a giant waterlily. Also cacti, carnivorous plants and fish.

A mangrove swamp, tropical montane zone, underground viewing aquaria … desert area … ferns, orchids, giant waterlily, cacti, succulents … carnivorous plants, begonias … not forgetting the popular … desert diorama.

The house was designed with the pleasure of visitors in mind

A computerised control centre ... carefully meters energy usage in the conservatory's ten environments.

Every aspect of glasshouse design has been completely rethought to take full advantage of modern technology to produce a house which is as efficiently functional as possible.

T-RANGE
(NO.7 TO NO.14)

Each room in the T-Range is hotter than
the next. The pallid face of a moth orchid
stares from an abandoned easel, and a
pair of stiff, paint-speckled shoes stick
out from beneath the potting bench. The
air is thick with turpentine and pollen —
heavy with mist and heat, and the sound
of deep, laboured breathing.

By the mid-1800s a jumble of mismatched conservatories had appeared
around Kew's first official glasshouse, the Great Stove. They were
tumbledown and not particularly attractive, and so Kew decided to replace them
with a modern development, at the time of its conception called the New Range.

Designed by horticultural builder, hot water apparatus manufacturer and
Chelsea-dweller Henry Osman, the T-Range was so-called because, when viewed
on a map or from above, it originally resembled a capital letter T, and consisted of
a series of compartments or rooms in which temperatures ranged from steamy to
cool. Eventually the T shape was obscured by later architectural additions.

The T-Range was completed in 1869. Each teak-timbered section was assigned
a number from 7 to 14 and once inside, visitors could pass freely from one room
to the next without leaving the building. Each room, or house, was hotter than
the last and included the Succulent House, Sherman Hoyt House, Pitcher Plant
House, Victoria Regia House and Orchid Houses.

The Succulent House, No.5, was 200 feet long and filled with fleshy plants
fetched from deserts and dry places — acid green euphorbias, spiny cacti, agaves

and aloes whose sticky insides oozed when accidentally snapped. In 1913 the century plant, the largest agave in the Gardens, produced a flower on a stalk 25 feet high, and had to be removed from the Succulent House to the lawn outside, where visitors flocked to see its giant splendour.

Perhaps the most fabulous of the rooms in the T-Range was No.7A, the Sherman Hoyt House, which included a generous gift from Minerva Sherman Hoyt, an American activist who was deeply interested in desert plants and spent much of her life trying to preserve their habitats. The House included a host of prickly specimens arranged in front of a curved canvas backdrop painted by a desert-loving American artist called Perry McNeely. This diorama featured Californian mountains and plants such as the smoke tree and creosote bush. Old red sandstone from Somerset was placed in front of the panorama, together with yellow Devonian sand, cacti and other juicy succulent plants, in an attempt to fool visitors into thinking they had, upon entering the House, passed through a portal and been temporarily transported to the golden west.

Inside House No.9A, the Pitcher Plant House, a collection of murderous flesh-eaters lay in wait. Suspended in teak baskets swinging from the roof, pitcher plants, vicious Venus flytraps and toothy sundews were poised, ready to snap shut and swallow their insect victims, devouring them slowly as they struggled in vain to escape.

EXTERIOR VIEW OF THE NEW T RANGE.

The Victoria Regia House, No.10, was much more serene, with beautiful lily pads floating on the surface of a tranquil pool.

A little further on, in Houses No.13 and 14, Kew's extensive orchid collection bloomed in the late winter, providing a glorious display of spectacular colours and fantastic shapes. The shrill whistling of Coqui the resident frog could often be heard coming from the leathery undergrowth. Painter Marianne North, who bequeathed to Kew her paintings and funded the Gallery to hang them in, liked to paint in the Orchid Houses, looking carefully at the strange flowers and capturing them on canvas. One day in 1911, however, the high temperature inside the stuffy glasshouse overcame her, and gardening staff found her under a bench where she had fainted in the heat.

The Houses which occupy the area to the east of the Rock Garden

A one-way system operates and entry is by the N. end at the base of the 'T'.

It comprises thirteen compartments, four of which are devoted to orchids; one to the Victoria regia, two to economic plants, the remainder to various stove and greenhouse plants.

So called because they were built in the form of a 'T'

From such artificial snuggeries it seems doubly dismal to turn out into the raw air of a truly British November.

ALOE HOUSE.

There should be time for a glance into the Succulent House, Number 5

A commodious structure … principally occupied by members of the cactus and aloe tribes, plants which, from their magnitude, and the imposing appearance of their pyramids of flowers, arrest the eye.

Entering the House by the north door, the visitor is confronted with the woody euphorbias in the centre bed and with smaller species in pots to the right and left.

A store of fleshy, scaly, spiky and prickly forms of cactus and aloe

There are specimens of agave, a sword-leafed plant which blooms once in seventy or eighty years.

The vegetation is remarkable for the grotesque forms it assumes, its fleshiness and succulency, its excessive armature of spines and prickles, and ... thick tough skin.

American plants

THIS HOUSE TOGETHER WITH THE SCENIC BACKGROUND AND MANY OF THE PLANTS WAS PRESENTED TO THE ROYAL BOTANIC GARDENS, KEW, BY Mrs SHERMAN HOYT OF PASADENA, CALIFORNIA HOUSE ERECTED 1931

Entering No. 7 by the north door one can pass to the left into the Sherman Hoyt Cactus House, No. 7A.

This House was most generously presented to the Gardens by Mrs Sherman Hoyt of Pasadena, California, to contain cacti and other Southwest American plants, which she had exhibited at the Chelsea Flower Show.

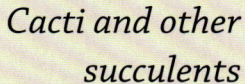

Cacti and other succulents

The present occupants of the house rise from the rock and sand in front of a very fine scenic painting of the Mojave Desert.

The whole exhibit in the Sherman Hoyt House is striking, pleasing, and, within its obvious limits, accurate as representing an American semi-desert area.

In the Number Nine Hothouse, there is the pitcher plant … Attracted by the bright colouring, the insect navigates and is lured on by the sweet-smelling nectar secreted by glands inside the pitcher. Buzzing round or slipping from the smooth rim … he generally falls plop into the watery fluid at the bottom. If he tries to climb out he is met by a series of hairs all pointing downward. So he flounders about until he is drowned. Then the pitcher plant can settle down to dinner … Sometimes the booby trap does not work and water insects, such as the mosquito, have been known to raise a family inside the carnivore's fat belly.

Growing in hanging baskets

Freaks of nature

Sundews ... catch and digest small insects by means of sticky glandular hairs.

Venus flytrap leaves are sensitive and catch insects by closing upon them. The proteins of their prey are then digested by means of a ferment secreted by special glands, and the leaves reopen when the process of digestion is complete.

The English common bladderwort ... gulps in insects ... In about twenty minutes the victim is no more.

VICTORIA REGIA HOUSE
VICTORIA HOUSE (NO.10)

One of the vegetable wonders of the world

The giant waterlily of the Amazon, named after Queen Victoria, is accommodated in a large rectangular tank.

The Victoria regia is remarkable for the size and strength of its leaves which, on the lower side, are provided with stout ribs and long sharp spines. The plant is an annual at Kew and flowers in the late summer.

It has a large tank for tropical aquatic plants in which is grown the giant waterlily.

The large flowers, which open in the evening, are at first white and gradually turn to purply pink before fading; they remain expanded for about 24 hours.

The largest known waterlily

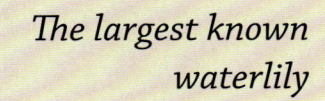

Most of them are dangling

The wonderful family represented here is now much the most popular of hot-house plants ... The extraordinary, often grotesque shapes the flowers assume combined with a frequently rich, brilliant or bizarre colouring, have always made them as interesting to the general public as they are to the botanist and horticulturist.

The most curious, the most abnormal of all plants; the whole tribe is, so to speak, out of rule. They are not dwellers on the earth as other plants are; they scorn to draw their sustenance from the vulgar mould ... but, adhering by their roots to the branches of living trees, they spread their fleshy leaves and wave their fantastic flower-spikes high in the air, deriving their nourishment from its rains and dews alone.

Here are billeted the delicate orchids, living on moist warm air

Their peculiar charm lies in their singular and fantastic forms, often most strangely imitative of other objects, as well as in their beauty, their fragrance, and their unusual manner of growth.

Wander with observant eye through these green alcoves; especially in the first opening of spring, when the majority of species are pushing into flower. Specimens may indeed be seen in blossom, on any and every day in the year.

TEMPERATE HOUSE

Men build a scaffold, shouting to one
another over the whirr of mechanical tools
and clanking metal. When they leave, the
glasshouse is quiet, still. As the light fades,
birds fly in through broken panes, seeking
roosts — flitting above old palms and cycads,
wrapped corpse-like in their plastic shrouds.

It took forty years to build the mammoth Temperate House — Kew's great glass cathedral, a crystal palace filled with the rarest of plants.

By 1859 Kew's green collections had become so multitudinous they had begun to crowd other glasshouses, piercing holes in fragile roofs as they scrambled for light. A new home had to be built, and so construction began. The centre block, or Winter Garden, as it was known, was finished first, followed by the octagons on either end.

As soon as the last labourer left the Gardens, barely before the window putty had set, stifled plants from the Palm House and some unhappy citrus trees from the Orangery emigrated to their new, roomy lodgings. Other Temperate House plants included monkey puzzles, tree ferns, rhododendrons, acacias, camellias and magnolias. Visitors, who were first admitted in 1863, were enthralled, passing back and forth along the paved pathways in long rustling skirts, gasping at the sheer size of some of the specimens, becoming lost in this vast indoor jungle.

More than another 30 years passed before Kew found the funds to complete the glasshouse. The southern section, known as the Mexican House, finally opened in 1897 and its northern counterpart, the Himalayan House — which featured rockpools — was completed before the end of the century. A teak extension was added to the west side of the north octagon in 1925 and lasted over 50 years.

Human visitors were not the only creatures to enjoy the luscious plants in the glasshouse. In the 1890s they were beset by plagues of pests. To combat them, gardeners tried saturating the soil with a mustard spray, alas to no avail. However, they had more luck with potatoes, which they used to lure wireworm into buckets of paraffin, and they also climbed up high to coat the heads of the tallest palms and yuccas with an insecticide made from oil and soft soap.

During the Second World War the Temperate House was badly damaged by bomb blasts. In 1941, thousands of panes of glass were smashed in minutes. A million splinters covered the flowerbeds, pots and borders throughout the building, and many plants were ripped to ribbons by shards of glass. As winter approached, many specimens were lost to the frost and chilly winds that snuck in through broken panes.

In 1970, when elderly panes of glass again began to fall from the roof, the building had to be closed to visitors on windy days for fear of decapitating them, and gardening staff had to wear hard hats. Consequently, a huge restoration was undertaken later that decade. Most of the plants were removed from the building, but an enormous Chilean wine palm stayed behind, wrapped in polythene. The reopening party in 1982 included a string quartet and fireworks.

A further restoration was completed in 2018 and visitors to the glasshouse can now enjoy breathing the same air as over 10,000 plants.

THE TEMPERATE HOUSE ROYAL BOTANIC GARDENS, KEW.

If time permits, go to the big Temperate House

This house perhaps appeals to the imagination as much as any other part of Kew.

The Temperate House is ... used for the display of large specimens of hardy flowering plants and shrubs, which, when grouped amongst the most luxuriant verdure, make this house the most effective and beautiful at Kew.

Trees and shrubs from far flung parts

THE TROPICAL HOUSES, KEW GARDENS.

The most pleasant of all the greenhouses at Kew at any season of the year, for it is kept at a "comfortable" temperature, is roomy, is provided with seats, and there are always interesting plants to see in it.

It is divided into three distinct portions, which are united together by two octagonal buildings.

WINTER GARDEN (CENTRAL SECTION)

One passes into the Winter Garden or central section. In this building, of which the apex of the roof is 60 feet above the ground, trees of considerable size can be grown, and a glance will show that full advantage has been taken of this opportunity.

A cool oasis in summer beneath tree ferns, palms and tall trees

Because of the tall trees and the birds singing and flying about, the central section gives the impression of a rather damp dark woodland. This impression is added to by the tree ferns and creepers which grow so well here.

A haven of greenery and delicate blooms in winter

No house of plants in Kew is, on the whole, so charming and uniformly agreeable as this. In cold, wintry weather ... the change from the bleak outside, with its lifeless trees and perhaps biting wind, to the soft, still air and richly luxuriant vegetation of the Winter Garden is always delightful. In the torrid heat of July and August, on the other hand, when one is apt to look askance at any glass-house, it is frequently cooler here than out-of-doors. It is a type of greenhouse which probably gives greater pleasure with less cost than any other.

HIMALAYAN HOUSE (NORTHERN SECTION)

The northern portion, known as the Himalayan House, is mainly devoted to tender rhododendrons from the Himalayas and to camellias. The majority of these plants will not stand the winter at Kew … in the open.

Immediately inside the door are two pools, one on each side of the path, in which waterlilies … are grown, and some interesting water plants grow around the margin.

Some very beautiful climbers are to be seen in this house, trained upon the roof supports or climbing up the walls.

Species native of the Himalaya

This house is at its best from February to May

MEXICAN HOUSE (SOUTHERN SECTION)

Passing through the southern octagon, which is filled with a collection of different varieties of orange and lemon trees, the southern or Mexican portion of the Temperate House is reached.

On either side of the door will be seen handsome specimens of the elegant Mexican Palm.

Plants of warm, temperate countries

Desert plants

The Mexican House, though containing many plants from Mexico, is not wholly confined to a representation of the plants of that country.

At last, the flowers show their vermicelli
crowns. Huge blooms are ripe and ready
— their heady perfume sticks to the air.
The moon watches through the glass
roof as a gardener moves methodically
round the pool, dabbing her brush in
the crystalline pollen which reminds
her of childhood sherbet.

The Waterlily House is Kew's hottest, most humid environment. Waterlilies were first grown at Kew in the 1850s, and were so instantly popular with visitors that a special house was constructed to accommodate these round plant platters, floating on the surface of the circular pool.

Overhead, cucumbers, calabashes and loofahs trail their drapery, dangling from the pitched roof like hanged men. Convolvulus writhes its tendrils over the pool railing, strangling the metal.

The water in the pool is heated. Once, goldfish lived briefly in the water, but it was too hot for them, and cooked them overnight.

The lily seeds are sown deep in the winter. By July, the leaves are huge. In years gone by, gardening staff would demonstrate their strength by climbing atop them and posing for photographs.

The lily flowers smell of pineapple. They open at night, ghost white under the moon, which haunts the sky above. In nature, the waterlily is pollinated by a midnight beetle, but at Kew, gardeners stay up late and gently tickle the dusty flowers with the bristles of a paintbrush, transferring powdery pollen from one bloom to the next.

A little building near the Palm House

Passing through a vestibule, where we see the hot-water pipes, which maintain the requisite temperature both of air and water for the health and vigour of this denizen of an equatorial clime, we enter through a glass door which must not be left open.

The centre of the room is occupied by a circular tank thirty-six feet in diameter, on whose tepid water float the grand salver-shaped leaves of the noblest flower ever discovered.

An unpretending, but roomy and commodious stove

During the summer, the leaf of the plant at Kew is usually inverted, so that visitors may see its marvellous construction.

Everything grows with great rapidity and luxuriance in the hot, steamy atmosphere.

Author S. Goldney's unofficial guidebook from 1907 showing the Palm House.

1979 guidebook showing the Palm House, Pond and one of the Kylins.

THE

ROYAL BOTANIC GARDENS

KEW

THE PALM HOUSE

KEY PLAN

PRICE : Ninepence Net.

1963 fold-out map showing the Palm House.

The Princess of Wales
CONSERVATORY

Commemorative guidebook from 1987 to celebrate the new Princess of Wales Conservatory.

BRICK & STONE

The Kew of the late eighteenth century was dotted over with a strange assortment of buildings

From humble tool sheds, stables and cloakrooms to grand edifices such as Kew Palace and the Orangery, Kew's landscape has always been studded with buildings.

Completed in 1631, Kew's oldest surviving structure is Kew Palace, one of three palaces built in the Gardens. Previously, the royal family also lived in a very large building known as the White House, which stood on the lawn in front of Kew Palace — the grand old plane tree there once grew against the White House walls, which were eventually demolished in 1802. Kew's third palace was an absurd castellated structure, topped with turrets and crenelated battlements overlooking the Thames, on the site of the current car park. It was torn down, unfinished, in 1829.

Much is written in the Gardens' guidebooks of the surviving Palace, a building considered so important that Kew also published several monograph guidebooks focusing solely on the house and its contents. The Palace — often known as the Dutch House owing to its gabled, continental style — was built on the site of a 16th-century dwelling called the Dairy House. As explained in the 1951 guidebook: "the Dairy House was pulled down and the only remnant of it which remains is a Gothic crypt, with a vaulted roof, beneath the present building". The Palace was then constructed above this ancient cellar by a prosperous merchant called Samuel Fortrey, whose legacy is commemorated, as detailed in the 1956 guide to the Palace, "by the initials and date ... which surmount the main entrance". Above the Palace doorway are carved the letters F, S and C — a permanent reminder of its original occupants: Samuel and his wife Catherine.

After a time, Kew Palace and the White House were leased by the royal family and Kew became a favourite home of Princess Augusta, mother of George III. Augusta, who was very much interested in botany, is credited with founding the Gardens, and spent a great deal of money on plants and buildings for the landscape. She employed the architect William Chambers, described by author Nowell Hall in the unofficial guidebook *The Romance of Kew — History, Guide, Map and Pictures of the Gardens* (published in 1966) as "a man of imagination" who, "given a free hand, made the most of his opportunity". Chambers is responsible for several of Kew's extant buildings, including the Great Pagoda, the Ruined Arch, the Temple of Aeolus and the Orangery, as well as a great many more which no longer survive. A guide celebrating the Orangery published in the 1970s reveals that "to please Princess Augusta, Chambers published in 1763 a large work showing 'Plans, Elevations, Sections and Perspective Views of the Gardens' ". The 1970s Orangery guide also explains that this building was built "to the design of William Chambers" and that he had used an innovative building technique:

> At superficial glance it appears to be of stone but it is actually built of brick, covered with Chambers' own very durable brand of stucco and rusticated to produce the effect of stone. The design obtains its charm from the well-balanced proportions and the linear pattern formed by the channels in the stucco and the bars of the windows.

Although inventive in design, the Orangery, originally intended as a home for citrus trees, did not admit enough light and the plants inside struggled. Therefore, as described in the 1970 guidebook,

> having been used as a greenhouse for 100 years, it was turned into a timber museum in the 1860s and remained as such until it was turned back into an Orangery in 1959, when it was reopened by HM the Queen on the occasion of the bicentenary of the Gardens.

Finally, in 1989 the Orangery was transformed into a refectory and has remained so ever since.

In the 1700s of course, there were no cafés at Kew, but other buildings in the Gardens were associated with refreshments. The first of these is the Ice House, where winter ice from the Pond was stored so that the royal family could enjoy cooling drinks in the summer months. As explained in the 1979 guidebook, "it is not known exactly when the Ice House was built" but the north wall of the entrance tunnel is part of the boundary wall of the original garden, and it certainly feels very old.

The royal family frequently used Queen Charlotte's Cottage as a picnicking retreat. As detailed in the 1930 guidebook, this rustic cottage hidden in Kew's deep dark woods was "built about 1760 by George III and used by him and Queen Charlotte as a summer tea-room". On walks from Kew Palace, the royal party would gather in the upstairs room where they would be served delicious morsels. A 1956 guide describes the fabulous interior,

> which has painted wall decoration of considerable charm and interest. It is evidently intended to give to the whole interior the appearance of a tent, even the plaster ceiling being shaped to simulate the billowing of canvas. The walls have at intervals paintings of bamboo uprights, up which swarm climbing plants, among which the convolvulus predominates.

Another fairy-tale building set within the Kew landscape is the Campanile, a romantic, Italianate chimney from which it is perfectly easy to imagine a princess waving. In truth, its purpose is much more functional than folkloric — it was built to carry away smoke from the boilers beneath the Palm House, as explained in the 1858 guidebook:

> To avoid the unsightliness of a chimney attached to, or even placed near, so noble a structure, the smoke is conveyed by underground flues, within a brick tunnel ... to a distance of 479 feet from the House; where a shaft or ornamental tower is erected, 96 feet in height.

Kew's brick and stone buildings are special places because the memory of the people who lived and worked within them is mixed into the mortar that holds them together. These are the places that people who knew and loved the Gardens lived in, picnicked in and climbed up. These are the places whose foundations are buried deep within Kew's soil.

CAMPANILE
CHIMNEY SHAFT
WATER TOWER

Beneath the Palm House parterres, the echo of
the ghost railway sounds in the tunnel — wheels
rattle on the track, down in the darkness.
The Campanile keeps watch, a stiff sentinel
surveilling the night, staring at the sky, as black
as the smoke that once crawled up its throat.

The pretty Palm House parterres hide a secret labyrinth: an underground matrix of tunnels, subterranean passages leading from the glasshouse to the tall, butter-coloured chimney that stands across the lawn.

Kew's Campanile was built in the middle of the 19th century, at the same time as the Palm House, for its purpose is entwined with the glasshouse where palms were kept warm using coal-burning boilers. Sacks of sooty fuel were loaded directly into the Palm House basement using an underground railway that shuttled through the tunnels, and when the coal was burnt, smoke from the furnaces curled furtively through the brick-lined passages, weaving its serpentine way to the tower, rising up and out through the holes in its turret.

Campanile means 'bell tower' in Italian, and Kew's Romanesque ziggurat certainly evokes Mediterranean piazze, where the sound of cracked bells rings out over paved concourses, bleached shining white by the sun. Kew's minaret, however, never contained a belfry — only a water tank, hammer-beaten from welded metal. This lofty reservoir harnessed gravity's pressure and the power of a steam pump to send water down the tower to sprinklers in the Palm House, creating artificial rain showers that drizzled over the plants.

ROSES IN THE ITALIAN GARDEN, KEW GARDENS.

A shaft of much architectural beauty

The Shaft or Campanile now comes into view; it is covered with ivy for about three-quarters of its height.

The Campanile, or Water Tower, near the Victoria Gate, was … intended as a smoke shaft for the Palm House furnaces, to which it is connected by an underground passage. A reservoir was also connected at the top to give sufficient pressure for the palms, &c., to be watered overhead. It no longer serves either of these purposes, but makes a pleasing architectural feature.

A lofty ornamental chimney, in the vicinity of the Palm House, for supplying the stoves with water and carrying off the smoke to a distance, so that it may neither injure the plants nor interfere with the harmony and verdure of the Gardens.

A very handsome tower

SHAFT OF THE GREAT PALM-STOVE.

ICE HOUSE
ICE WELL

The Queen turns her head to pinpoint
the almost imperceptible sound she has
heard — the faint, delicious crystal clink
of ice in a glass. She lifts the drink from
the tray she is brought, smiling at the idea
of swallowing the Pond, of consuming
part of the landscape she loves.

Hidden under a mound where badgers like to dig, plunged fathoms into the primordial earth, the Ice House lurks: a brooding, sarcophagal chamber topped with dense evergreen shrubbery that casts its shade over the tomb.

Kew's Ice House was used by the royal family during the hot, hazy summers of the 1700s. Servants would fetch crushed ice from the Well to cool long drinks and chill soft, sweet puddings which they brought wobbling to the dining room.

Filling the Ice House was never a popular job, and those who undertook this task had to be bribed with gallons of beer. In the depths of winter a gang of men used savage saws that chewed the frozen surface of the Pond; they hacked huge cubes and loaded them into carts for their horses to pull — the animals steamed and stamped, breathing hard in the brittle air.

At the Ice House solid chunks of Pond were lowered one by one down the brick-lined shaft and straw was sprinkled between each layer for insulation. After three days' cruel labour, the Well was finally full. The men slammed shut the heavy wooden door, trapping their icy prisoner inside.

Used when Kew belonged to the royal family

In the seventeenth, eighteenth and early nineteenth centuries, ice was harvested in winter, and stored in ice houses packed with straw to aid insulation. The ice was used mainly for cooling drinks and keeping food fresh in summer.

The north wall of the entrance tunnel is part of the boundary wall of the original garden.

Under the far side of the mound is an ice house

The princesses squabble over bedrooms, running flat-footed across the landing to see which has the best view. Their brother, tired of the bickering, takes a dusty chalk and prints their names on the wooden panelling above each door: Charlotte, Mary, Elizabeth.

This gorgeous, gabled dolls house was a much-loved retreat of George III, his wife Charlotte and their numerous brood, who escaped the hot, fetid city to spend summers by the lazy river, tending plants and climbing trees.

As well as inhabiting their red-brick home, the family also lived in the White House, a much larger building that stood in front of the Palace. It was demolished in 1802 owing to the King's dislike for its damp, fusty rooms, labyrinthine corridors and dark staircases.

The King loved the Palace best, for here he could live simply. Each morning, he would rise at half past seven and, after attending religious service, would breakfast with his family at nine. He liked riding horses through the Gardens, and would sometimes turn buttons on his lathe, play the harpsichord, and enjoy games of chess and backgammon with his sons and daughters. Evenings were spent dining on mutton and turnips, and playing cards as the princesses turned their needles, embroidering by candlelight up in their mother's Boudoir.

Other rooms in the Palace include the King's Breakfast Room, Library and the Queen's Drawing Room, where, in 1818 two of the princes were married on the same sweet July day.

Upstairs, the bedchambers were simply kept and furnished, with bed curtains of white dimity. The Prince of Wales took it upon himself to chalk the name of each of the bedroom's occupants above the doorframes.

The Palace passed from royal to government control in the 1800s, and at the end of that century it was partially opened as a museum, filled with royal relics — a silver rattle, smelling-bottles and snuff boxes, mantle clocks, fire irons and a chaise longue, cups, saucers, boot scrapers, candlesticks and lanterns. Visitors filed in to gawk at the vestiges of lives well lived.

A good and characteristic example of old English architecture

The best way of reaching Kew Palace is through the principal entrance to Kew Gardens on Kew Green.

The house itself, both outside and in … possesses sufficient antiquity and historical associations to render it decidedly worthy of a visit.

Let us now pursue the gravelled walk which leads ... towards the Palace

The brick is laid in Flemish bond (i.e. with the sides and ends of the bricks alternating) ... The brickwork shows great skill and artistry — one of the great features of the house is, indeed, the brickwork ornamentation such as the rustication around the windows.

Kew is the smallest of the Royal Palaces — so small, indeed, that it barely had room for the King and Queen who lived there: King George III and Queen Charlotte.

ORANGERY

It is dim in the Orangery. Sour perfume
hangs in the air, dirty and dark. Footsteps
sound on the flagstone floor as someone
moves through the building unseen,
hidden by dense forest foliage. Trees rasp
their glossy leaves against the windows,
desperately seeking the sun, struggling to
make bitter fruits in its image.

Above the ostentatious doorways of the Orangery, under the peaked roofs,
a giant, florid letter A is carved into an elaborate cartouche — A for
Augusta, mother of George III, who commissioned her champion Swedish-
Scottish architect William Chambers to design and construct the building for
her precious citrus trees.

Chambers set to work on this five-year project in 1757, building it from brick
and covering the front elevation with his own special brand of stucco to make
it look like stone. Chambers never gave away his secret stucco recipe, but it is
thought to be a mixture of stone, lime and sharp sand.

When the building was completed in 1761, the oranges, together with their
lemony relatives, took up residence, but alas, theirs was a dark and dismal
home that suited them very badly, and made them miserable. Despite the huge
windows, not enough light reached the trees and they soon began to perish.
To combat this, the outlines of additional glazed doors were chalked out on the
brickwork at either end of the building, and these new openings were knocked
out of the walls. But still the plants did not flourish. Eventually, they were moved
to Kensington Palace Orangery and down to the Temperate House.

Empty of fruit trees, Kew put the Orangery to a variety of alternative uses. From 1863 to 1959 it was Museum Number Three, the Timber Museum. It was then renovated, restored to its original function as a citrus house and reopened by Her Majesty Queen Elizabeth II. From 1972 it became an exhibition area and bookshop, until in 1989 the building became a tea room. In 2002 it was altered again and opened as a restaurant.

Beautifully proportioned

Originally intended for orange trees

The attention is drawn by a large edifice … which we still call by its original name … the Orangery.

The Orangery can be seen through the trees ahead … it is regarded as a very fine example of Georgian architecture.

The largest classical-style building in the Gardens.

Orangeries were almost essential accessories … for not only were they necessary greenhouses for the orange trees, but also places of promenade in bad weather. In summer, however, the orange trees, which were grown in tubs, were set outside.

QUEEN CHARLOTTE'S COTTAGE
QUEEN'S COTTAGE

Spiders listen at the doorway, eavesdropping on the mice, spinning squeaked stories into cobwebs. Woodpigeons coo love songs down the chimney — soft notes gather in the pleats of the mildewed curtains and hide behind the ragged pelmets. In the upstairs parlour, painted flowers creep over the rotten ceiling.

Kangaroos, pretty partridges, an antelope, pheasants, a buffalo, an elk, springbok and gazelle, a pair of black swans, exotic cattle and a colossal tortoise all lived in this wild area of the Gardens in the 1700s. Kept by the royal family in paddocks and pens, the animals provided outlandish interest for those taking long walks from Kew Palace, who would peer into their cages, breathing the musky, dung-heavy scent, feeding them fruits and grasses.

The menagerie keeper, who looked after the beasts, lived in the small cottage nearby, until Queen Charlotte, wife of George III, demanded that the dwelling be enlarged — and so the building became a place where the royal family would take refreshment when visiting their bizarre zoo.

Under the rye-thatched roof, they would sit in the upstairs picnic room, enjoying long lunches and delicate afternoon teas served on crockery painted with flowers. The Cottage was a favourite place of Queen Charlotte's daughters, and Princess Elizabeth is thought to have painted the wreaths of convolvulus and nasturtium climbing the walls.

The last great tea party held in the Cottage took place in 1818, on the occasion of the double wedding of two of the princes. In Queen Victoria's time it was used as a summerhouse and shooting box, and her chaplain also held a three-day bazaar in the building in aid of a new vicarage.

At the end of the 1800s the Cottage was bequeathed to Kew by Queen Victoria. It lay untouched and abandoned, locked up for many years. Rabbits hopped across the doorstep and colonised the lawn. The sun faded the chintz curtains sagging sadly at the lattice windows, and moths devoured the velvet cushions. Creepers crept over the brickwork, affording the building a tired, romantic air.

The Cottage is now open in summer months when visitors are permitted to climb the curved staircase and look out into the wild Cottage Wood.

Picturesque thatched cottage

Its deep eaves, small windows and thatched roof pose obligingly for the camera.

Romantically-minded engaged couples have no doubt cast longing eyes upon the cottage, roofed with a thick covering of thatch and embowered in ivy.

A romantic old house

A favourite summerhouse of King George III … Here the royal family often took tea, at times breakfast and occasionally dinner.

Dreaming among the trees and spring flowers, it seems to be peopled by the ghosts of the royal children who once played there.

Guidebook from the 1970s celebrating the Orangery.

The ORANGERY

ROYAL BOTANIC GARDENS
KEW

Kew Palace

MINISTRY OF WORKS OFFICIAL GUIDE.   PRICE 1s. 6d. NET.

1956 guidebook for Kew Palace, published by the Ministry of Works,
the government body responsible for the Palace at the time.

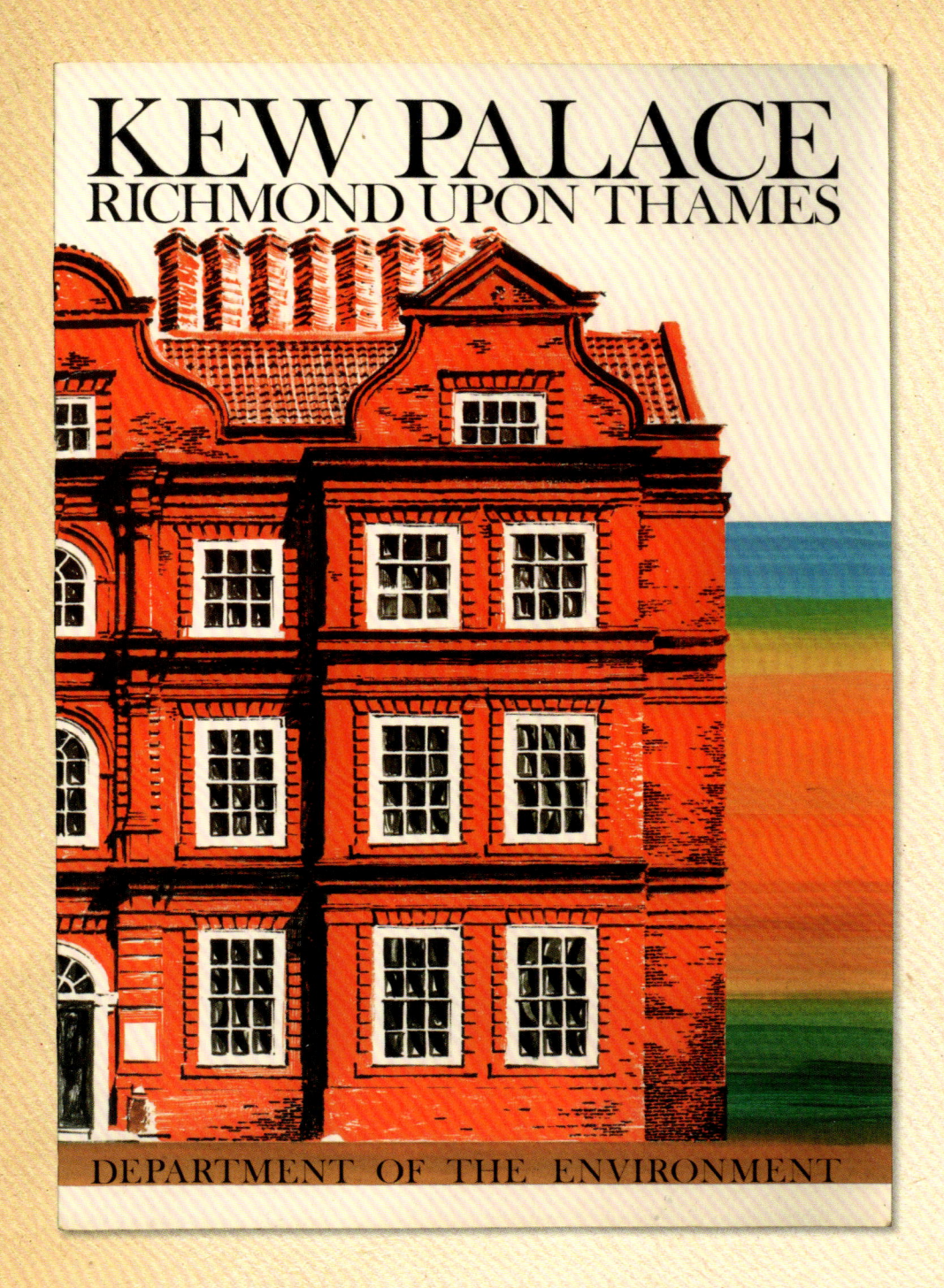

KEW PALACE
RICHMOND UPON THAMES

DEPARTMENT OF THE ENVIRONMENT

1983 guidebook for Kew Palace, published by the Department of the Environment,
the government body responsible for Kew at the time.

WATER

Water can add greatly to the
attraction of a garden

Water surrounds the Gardens. The slow, silty Thames slides languidly past the western edge of Kew, embracing it, separating it from the parish of Brentford on the far bank, perpetuating its entity: water has literally shaped the landscape.

The river and the Gardens are old friends. Were it not for the river, the Gardens would not be. As detailed in the 1967 guidebook, "The Gardens lie on a flood plain terrace of the river Thames. The soil consists of river gravels and sand at least 30 feet deep, overlying the London clay".

The river once flowed into the Gardens, blurring the boundary between land and water, soaking the turf and turning it from riverbank to lagoon. As author Nowell Hall recalled in the unofficial guidebook, *The Romance of Kew — Where Flowers Always Bloom* (published in 1950): "the Pond was originally a swollen curve in a backwater of the Thames". Indeed, before its containment through embanking in 1847, the pond was previously much bigger and at one time drenched six acres of land. It was so large, in fact, that it was known as the Lake and contained a three-acre island.

Kew is named for the water — in 1327 it was baptised 'Cayho', a liquid elision of 'kai', a landing place or quay, and 'ho' a spur of land, formed by the river bend. On this bend where water and time slow, nobility and royalty chose to make their riverside homes, including, of course, Kew Palace. The scenery was charming, bucolic, and transport along the river into London was easily found.

Indeed, before the coming of the railway and affordable motor transport, taking a riverboat to Kew was the optimum way to travel. Into the middle of the 1900s, Kew had two riverside gates: Brentford Gate, which afforded visitors access not only from the car park as it does now, but also from the Brentford ferry; and Isleworth Gate, through which visitors walking along the river towing path could enter the Gardens.

Kew now has several bodies of water, yet only the Pond is natural, fed by an underground spring. The first of the others to be created was the Lake, formed, as explained in a guidebook published in 1971, "from existing marshy ground and gravel pits". It was dug in 1856 and filled for the first time in 1861. The alluvium removed from the pit was barrowed across the Gardens and compacted to form the mound beneath the Temperate House. Many of Kew's original paths were also made from this gravel.

Seventeen years later, Kew's newest water feature was the Aquatic Garden, a large, brick-lined tank near to Museum Number Two, which was originally oriented east–west, but replaced in 1909 with the existing seven tanks which lie north–south.

In 1897 the Waterlily Pond was dug at the edge of Cedar Vista for tender aquatic plants such as waterlily and iris, which grew abundantly in the warm waste water and condensed steam fed from a nearby pumping station.

Much is made in the guidebooks of the inhabitants of these bodies of water; as explained in the 1912 edition: "On the Pond in front of Museum No. 1 and on the Lake towards the river, are a collection of swans, geese, and ducks."

Over centuries, Kew's watery places have provided a home to swans, geese, ducks, moorhen, cranes, storks, and even pelicans and penguins. In turn, visitors have flocked to the Gardens to spot these popular birds, before mimicking the seagulls featured in the 1938 guidebook, and taking "their departure every evening about sunset."

AQUATIC GARDEN

The shoal flashes and turns, darting
into the safe, dark shelter of a lily pad,
hiding from the winged shadow circling
overhead. The sun fills the pool with
liquid light, turning a torch on scaled,
bright beams weaving through swaying
underwater forests, as a fast, cruel beak
breaks the surface, snaps, and swallows.

Kew's old Aquatic Garden was a single rectangular, brick-lined sunken tank, built in 1873 and oriented in parallel to the nearby Museum Number Two. In 1909, it was replaced with the more stylish design that still survives today, now oriented north–south.

When first installed, the large, oval-shaped tank and six surrounding others were christened 'White City' because they were so boxy and white. London's White City, from whence the Aquatic Garden's nickname originated, was the location for several exhibitions, and got its name from the marble cladding on the exhibition pavilions. One of the exhibitions was the 1910 Japan–British Exhibition, of which the Japanese Gateway is a legacy.

Integral hot water pipes gave plants growing in the Aquatic Garden tanks the best chances in the often inclement British weather, and waterlilies, lotus, sedges, rushes and rare marsh plants flourished there.

Goldfish living in the pools were not so lucky — a seagull is reported to have devoured whole shoals of them in 1910.

A sunken, formal area near the Iris Garden

The Aquatic Garden consists of a large central sunken tank, which can be warmed by means of hot-water pipes, filled with the different varieties of white, yellow, and red water lilies. The corner tanks are at a higher level so that their contents can be examined with ease.

Waterlilies and goldfish

Parallel with the main tank are two beds for British marsh plants, some of which are rare.

LAKE

The wind blows the Lake into a fine, grey spray. On the islands, swamp cypresses stand at the water's edge, grasping the banks with knobbly old toes. The river pours through the culvert, coating their bunions with sticky mud, wrapping them in bandages of green weed.

Once, the land from which the Lake is hollowed was open heath — a wide, flat place, where, in the 1700s, a strange building could be found emerging from the earth amongst the wild yellow broom and prickly gorse. Merlin's Cave was thatched and resembled an eccentric haystack. A poet called Stephen Duck could often be found within, running his bony fingers over his vellum-bound library and weaving his verse for the tableau of waxwork figures that lived in the Cave: Merlin, Queen Elizabeth I, Minerva, and others. It was demolished in 1766.

Nearly a century later, the designs for the Temperate House were drawn, and it was decided to elevate the glasshouse from the surrounding landscape by building it on a huge, rectangular plinth, thereby enhancing its majesty. The gravel for this plinth was dug from the scrubby plain in the middle of Kew's estate, and so the Lake came into being.

An underground culvert known as the crocodile was channelled out of the earth, connecting the newly grubbed crater with the river beyond the Gardens' edge, and in 1861, as the sea tide washed upstream, murky, frothing water gushed into the Lake for the first time, roaring through the sluice gate and flooding the land.

As the moon dragged tide after tide into the Gardens, the water in turn pulled dirty old mud from the riverbank into the Lake, clogging the bottom. In the early 1800s, an extra gang of men specially hired to remove the mud swelled Kew's staff. They wheeled out ten thousand cartloads of squelchy filth dredged from the Lake floor and spread it across the landscape, scooping it over the roots of beech and horse chestnut to help them grow.

Afterwards, the appearance of the Lake surface was much improved — it was cleaner and brighter, and the planting of alders, white willows, waterlilies, daffodils and Japanese primrose enhanced the beauty of the banks — so much so that two painters, Georgina and Constant de L'Aubinière, spent two years *en plein air*, catching various views of the ornamental water in their brush bristles and daubing them on paper. The paintings were exhibited in the Marianne North Gallery and also published in an album in 1897.

Several masses protrude from the Lake; there are four densely wooded islands, which turn fiery red in autumn — flaming votives alight on the water. In 1975, following the demolition of old London Bridge during the previous decade, four large blocks of Cornish granite taken from the crossing were dumped in the Lake as a feeding platform for waterfowl.

THE LAKE, KEW GARDENS   57109

KEW GARDENS. The LAKE

Many charming views may be discovered by traversing its banks

This beautiful feature of Kew, which covers four and a half acres, is entirely artificial, and up to about 1845 the area now occupied by water was of the same level as the surrounding land. There are some 15 or 16 miles of paths in Kew, and much of the material to make them was excavated from the site of the Lake; about 1859 a further large quantity was taken to form the raised terrace on which the Temperate House was afterwards built.

*The largest sheet
of water within the
Gardens is the Lake*

The Lake Kew Gardens

The river is ... the sole source of supply, but water can only be obtained at high tide; usually at new and full moon.

Its wild look has resulted from decades of growth. Here, in addition to the weeping willows and other trees, are English marsh plants and flowers such as Michaelmas daisies, Chinese asters and red-hot pokers.

POND

The ice is thick enough for skating. Out on
the frosted surface, the flames of a brazier
breathe in the darkness, embers sparking
against the hard air. The twisted fingers of an
elm are bundled for kindling — they reach
into the fire, gnarled green, hissing.

The Pond is older than the Gardens. Hundreds of years ago, it was much
larger: a swampy place, a creek, a backwater of the Thames, a score of lagoons
washed by water from the river and filled by underground springs.

Years later, to celebrate George III's seventeenth birthday, the royal family
sailed across the pond in a boat shaped like a giant swan, named after his mother,
Augusta.

The pond wall was built in 1847, the waters bricked up using remnants from
demolished glasshouses. Half a century later, the Pond's winter ice would grow so
thick that gardeners would skate on it in the evenings.

Around the same time, when a visitor plunged from the wall into the icy water
below, a gardener named Fishlock — on his way back from lunch — dived in and
saved a life.

The following year, a black swan — who had been known as the Swashbuckler
of the Pond for his terrorising of the pelicans and peacocks — was not so lucky, and
met death in the jaws of a fox. The fox was not the only creature to steal wildlife
from the pond: at 5am on a Sunday morning in August 1961 a constable caught
two men with fishing tackle and a large carp they had taken from the water.

A handsome piece of water with a jet or small fountain, enlivened by swans

An ornamental piece of water, on whose banks weeping willows lave their drooping branches, and on whose placid bosom float proudly the swans and other aquatic birds that have been from time to time presented to the Gardens.

*The fish in the pond include
eel, carp, roach and dace*

The south-western end and part of the two adjoining sides of the pond are faced with
brick and over them trail festoons of rambler roses which add much to the attractions
of the pond in summer.

The pond contains large numbers of fish … some of which grow to considerable size.
Periodically it is net dragged and the tubs of fish caught are taken away to the Thames
… or to the London Zoo.

WATERLILY POND
LILY POND

Six o'clock. Bells ring from the church on the Green, mixing with the smell of mown grass. Abel Watford, greasy from a day at the pumps, washes himself in the chipped messroom sink. He climbs into whites that glow against his tan, claps together his huge, leather-gloved hands, and takes an evening stroll to the cricket pitch.

This is where the peacocks live, down at the bottom of the Gardens. They strut majestically down Cedar Vista, swishing their tail feathers like Victorian bustles. At the Waterlily Pond, they look down into the water, admiring their regal reflections.

The Waterlily Pond is a still, calm, enigmatic place, created in 1897, when it was dug out to make a pool in which to grow tender aquatic plants — white waterlilies, blue and yellow iris.

Some of the waterlilies were supplied by Lionel de Rothschild, an MP who adored plants. However, some of Kew's gardening staff did not share his enthusiasm. One day in 1956, they developed rashes on their arms as they thinned out the lilies. They had been attacked by parasitic worms and had to have penicillin injections.

A handsome white dovecote once stood by the water's edge. From their sheltered perches the birds looked out at the great leafy gunnera and swamp cypress overhanging the bank.

Blue-tailed damselflies can often be seen moving above the Waterlily Pond in high summer, hovering over the surface and resting on the lily leaves.

The water was originally heated with condensed steam from the local waterworks. A man called Abel Watford was in charge of the pumping machinery. He was a terrific cricketer, especially good at the wicket. When he was not looking after the pumps, he played for the Gardens team in matches against Kew Village.

A very charming picture from June onwards

In the Waterlily Pond ... waterlilies are seen to the greatest advantage at Kew, and it should be remembered that to see them at their best they should be examined in the morning when they are fully expanded.

The fine coloured waterlilies … are a conspicuous feature

The Water Lily Pond, Kew Gardens.

A collection of hybrid lilies is grown in the pond and gives a fine display in summer.

Supplied with condensed steam from the water-works; it is therefore possible to grow in it many half-hardy aquatics.

WATERFOWL

The Keeper fetches a clipboard from his office and strides towards the water, keen to make a start. The birds await him, cocking their heads and peering sideways as they recognise his silhouette. He takes the register, calling their names. Flocks float on the surface, black–green feathers coating the water like an oil-slick.

Wings and water

List of waterfowl living in the Gardens

With its several bodies of water, Kew seems to be a very inviting place for a water bird to build its nest, and generations of swans, geese and ducks have waded and waddled across the Gardens. Waterfowl feature in many of the guidebooks and the 1967 edition includes a register:

Abyssinian Geese

American Blue-winged Teal

Bar-headed Geese

Black Swans

Black-necked Swans

Canada Geese

Carolina Duck

Chinese Geese

Common Pochard

Egyptian Geese

European Shelduck

European Teal

Gadwall Duck

Gray Lag Geese

Magellan Geese

Muscovy Duck

Paradise New Zealand Shelduck

Pintail Duck

Red-crested Pochard

The Old Boathouse, Kew Gardens.

Birds have made their homes at Kew for centuries, boring holes in the trunks of giant redwoods in the Arboretum, pasting sticky daubed nests under the eaves of the Orangery, weaving reeds and grasses into a floating bower out on the Lake.

In the 1890s pelicans lived at Kew, ambling like old men, waiting for the Keeper to throw fish which they snapped in their beaks and choked down their stretchy gullets. Penguins, too, tumbled black-and-white at the water's edge — a favourite with children.

Kew's most famous avian resident was a handsome crane named Joey, also known as the Grand Old Man of the Gardens. Popular with visitors, he lived at Kew for over 20 years and was often to be found strutting around the Refreshment Pavilion.

Joey's life was eventful. He was the guardian of storks who were frequently attacked by geese, and had a love affair with a dainty female crane, having driven away her mate. Once, he lost his toe in the rotating blades of a motor mower. But this was not to be his only accident. On the last day of January 1935, he was found drowned in the Lake. It was presumed that in crossing from an island to the far bank, the thin ice beneath him had cracked and splintered, he had fallen and, unable to free himself, had felt the frozen fingers of death slowly tighten around his feathered throat.

That evening, newspaper placards across London proclaimed his demise. Kew replaced him two years later with another specimen, also called Joey.

Many beautiful wildfowl are to be seen. In the late afternoon the keeper whistles them for their tea. Arrowing their way, these smartest and most brightly coloured of fowl come streaming across the water to his call. For generations there has been a bond of friendship between the keepers and the children who throng the waterside … Asked nicely, the keeper is generally willing to name a prettily marked duck after young Thomas or William and more than one has been christened Junior after a small visitor from the United States.

The waterfowl move from Pond to Lake and Lake to Pond

Mallards, moorhens, coots and tufted ducks can usually be seen; these birds are not maintained by the Gardens but come and go as they please.

The ornamental waterfowl ... are a very popular feature with visitors, and the more confiding birds derive a considerable portion of their food from this source.

Unfortunately many birds have been lost ... owing to a severe outbreak of botulism. This disease occurs on muddy shallows around ponds and lakes and is most prevalent during hot weather. One of the main contributing factors to the development of this disease is believed to be the bread which is thrown into the water to feed the birds. Notices are therefore displayed asking visitors not to feed them.

Photographer E. J. Wallis's unofficial guidebook from 1900.

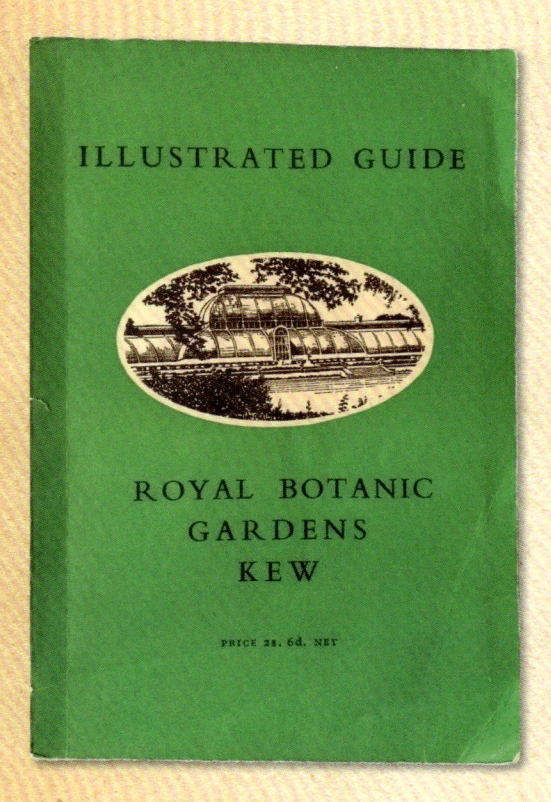

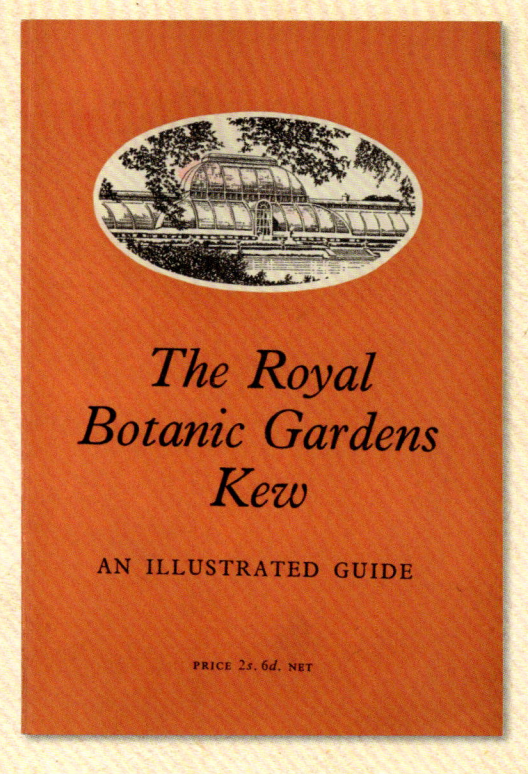

Guidebooks from 1951 (left) and 1959 (right) showing the Palm House and Pond.

THE PAGODA, KEW GARDENS

WONDER

A profusion of ... so-called temples ... scattered about the grounds, some of them very handsome structures

Much of Kew's landscape is laid out formally; visitors can easily navigate their way through it by following the lines of neatly trimmed borders and elegant parterres, and strolling down the wide, tree-lined vistas clearly marked on guidebook maps. However, there are wilder parts of Kew — those places in the dark pine woods and along the raggedy edges of the estate, down by the river — where it is quite easy to become disorientated. In these lesser-known parts of the Gardens follies serve as landmarks, and are described as such in several of the guidebooks. The 1951 edition details a common scenario, "The visitor unfamiliar with Kew will find certain features helpful to locate his position ... There are a number of structures which are of historic interest and which enable the visitor not sure of his surroundings to orientate himself."

Thus Kew's follies (together with smaller alcoves and shelters) serve a useful purpose for the visitor. This however, was not their initially intended function, which was, in fact, to serve no function at all.

Many of Kew's original follies — such as the Alhambra, the Gothic Cathedral and the Theatre of Augusta — were sprinkled through Kew's shrubberies and flower gardens in the 1700s for the pleasure of the royal family, who lived in Kew Palace at the time. The structures — described by author Nowell Hall in the unofficial guidebook *The Romance of Kew — History, Guide, Map and Pictures of the Gardens* (published in 1966) as "strange buildings" and "weird attractions" — reflected a contemporaneous trend in English garden design to include within a landscape gothic ruins, elegant temples, grottoes, hermitages and other exotic structures, for no purpose other than decadent ornamentation.

Kew's follies were embellished with gilding, bells, elaborate plaster friezes and dragons with wings of coloured glass; symbolic inscriptions were carved above doorways and octagonal roofs topped with shining finials. Ceilings supported by florid Corinthian columns were painted in the brightest blue and pierced with stars; classical statues loomed from crumbling arches; rich tapestries hung in scarlet rooms lit by golden lamplight — each building was more fantastically gorgeous and eccentric than the last.

Part of the follies' intrigue lies in their impermanence. Many of them were built deliberately as sham ruins, and some, such as the Palladian Bridge — built in one night from lath and plaster — were only ever intended to be temporary. Ultimately their contrived ephemerality was their literal downfall; as explained in the 1935 guidebook, many of them "fell into decay and were ultimately demolished".

Indeed, almost all of Kew's follies had disappeared by the time the first guidebook was introduced in 1847, but their powerful legacy clearly pervaded the authors' imaginations, and architecture in the landscape which could no longer be seen by late 19th- and 20th-century visitors was still detailed on the page.

Although the majority of Kew's follies have become history and legend, their physical impact can still be seen in the landscape. Many of them — such as the Mosque — were sited on small, specially created mounds. Whilst the temples and ruins have become faded memories, these hummocks remain. The follies have changed the shape of the Gardens forever.

Of the follies celebrated in this book, only the Temple of the Sun cannot now be found in the Gardens. It is included here because before it was destroyed in a storm in 1916, it was much vaunted in a number of the guidebooks as a glorious, blinding-white temple, gleaming in a circle of trees.

The others that remain — the Pagoda, the Ruined Arch, and assorted temples— give the Gardens, as explained in the 1966 guidebook, "their eighteenth century atmosphere": allowing the modern visitor to see Kew's history, shimmering through time.

Other wonderful things to be found in the Gardens and in the guidebooks include the Flagstaff, a mighty pole made from a single fir tree; sundials; and carved creatures — the Kylins and Queen's Beasts — who grin at one another across the Pond.

List of follies built in the Gardens

Kew's landscape was once crowded with curious buildings of all kinds. They added drama and intrigue to the landscape, and afforded visitors places to explore and to rest. The majority have now been dismantled, but they are remembered here:

Alhambra

Chinese Pavilion

Gallery of Antiques

Gothic Cathedral

Great Pagoda

Grecian Pavilion

House of Confucius

Japanese Gateway

King William's Temple

Menagerie

Mosque

Palladian Bridge

Queen's Pavilion

Ruined Arch

Temple of Aeolus

Temple of Arethusa

Temple of Bellona

Temple of Pan

Temple of Peace

Temple of Solitude

Temple of the Sun

Temple of Victory

Theatre of Augusta

FLAGSTAFF

Princess Mary Adelaide spreads puddles of
marmalade on thick slices of toasted bread,
gobbling them down as quickly as she can.
The day is tattering away and she is eager to
see the famous flagpole being raised. Later,
filled with indigestion and hiccoughing
into the wind, she watches, fascinated,
as the spar is heaved and hoisted.

Kew's flagstaffs are cursed. Each one tells a sorry story. The first was presented to the Gardens in 1856 by a timber trader called Edward Stamp. During its passage to Kew, it was towed up the Thames, where upon it was sliced in two by an aggressive tug boat. However, it was salvaged, spliced and sent to the Gardens, but whilst being hoisted the spar blew over, breaking into three useless logs.

On hearing the news, Stamp delivered a second tree. This was, at first, a successful specimen. Having been towed from Canada around Cape Horn to Britain, it was erected in 1861 near the Marianne North Gallery, on Victory Hill. Princess Mary Adelaide, wife of George V, wrote in her diary for that year that she had hurried to the Gardens immediately after breakfast to watch the Flagstaff being raised by shipwrights and sailors. It was 159 feet tall and crowned with a shining star.

However, by 1913 the pole had become riddled with dry rot and so was replaced with a third model in 1919, a 214-foot Douglas fir gifted by the government of British Columbia. This tree is named for botanist David Douglas, who died being gored to death by a bull. Alas, after some time, fungal rot was discovered by a steeplejack and the top of the pole was lopped off before being removed altogether.

Kew's final wooden Flagstaff was presented by the British Columbia Loggers' Association in 1959 — a giant at 225 feet. Its fate was sealed by the vicious beaks of a family of woodpeckers, who rendered it unstable, and in 2007 it was removed from the Gardens. Having learnt salutary lessons about the vagaries of wooden flagpoles, Kew now uses metal models.

This flagstaff may be seen far and near

A pole of Douglas fir

It is erected upon a mound, called Victory Hill, close to the North Gallery.

Gorse and broom and a wealth of different wild flowers stud the little hill on which the flagstaff stands.

Two young living specimens of Douglas Fir are to be seen on the slope to the north-west about 30 yards from the flagstaff.

A flag is hoisted on the birthdays of the various members of the royal family.

GREAT PAGODA

Magpies gather in the conifers, calling
out a warning. The air is ripe with a storm
which broods over the tower — grey–gold,
electric. Hanging from the highest rail, a
pocket watch glints and spins, counting
the minutes until the sky opens — ticking
in time with the thunder pulse, waiting
for the angry flash.

In the early 1800s, the view from the top of the Great Pagoda would have
included fields, market gardens and Marsh Gate Farm, where George III kept
his flock of merino sheep — tiny white specks, hundreds of feet below.

The Pagoda was built for a princess: Augusta, George's mother, over the winter
of 1761–2. Up and up it went, each of the ten storeys being expertly laid on top
of the next by a team of masons, led by principal bricklayer Solomon Brown.
Samuel Westcott covered the roofs with slate tiles, and Samuel Cobb painted
the tower in vivid colours: blue, red, white and green. Inside, carpenter George
Warren made the winding wooden staircase and Francis Engleheart skimmed the
walls with fresh plaster. All this labour was not inexpensive – the builders' bill
came to £12,000 — over one and a half million pounds today.

The folly was topped with a glowing golden finial and 80 dazzling dragons
crouched on the corners of the roofs. Carved from wood, they were coated in
shattered, iridescent glass which sparkled in the sun, and as the wind blew down
the vista, the tiny bells in their mouths tinkled their song across the Gardens.
By the 1780s, the dragons had been removed, as they had become badly degraded,
probably by the mini-ice age that crept over the land and destroyed the woodwork.

Nineteenth-century visitors were permitted to climb the Pagoda, and most descended again via the staircase. However according to legend, in the 1870s a man threw himself from the highest balcony. He hung his watch and chain on the railing before he jumped, and they were left, swinging in the wind, for several years afterwards.

Bombs, too, fell from the Pagoda's height — during the Second World War, British bombers tested the flight of their inventions by dropping model incendiaries through holes they drilled in each floor.

The Pagoda was restored to its former glory in 2018.

THE PAGODA, KEW GARDENS. D.636

There is perhaps no other building in the Royal Gardens which excites so much interest or evokes so many questions.

The building is a relatively simple structure … its interior, which is perfectly plain, contains nothing but the staircase, which communicates with the upper floors.

A garden ornament left over from a more elegant and spacious age

The Pagoda … serves so admirably as a landmark

The cedars near the Pagoda are all that remain of more extensive plantings. Unfortunately they tend to be short lived here, as they suffer from the polluted atmosphere of the London area.

JAPANESE GATEWAY
CHOKUSHI-MON

Animals splinter out of the carved
wood, galloping across the grain —
gouged in a workshop far away, where
sawdust floats in the citrus air and curled
shavings fall to the sunlit floor. Where,
carefully, Wada Genyemon turns his
tools to tease from the wood the story
his mother once told him.

At the end of Holly Walk the small hump of Mossy Hill pimples out of the
ground. It is named not for any green carpet, but rather for the Mosque, a
remarkable building which stood nearby in the 1700s. Topped by three ornate
domes and a shining crescent moon, its interior was rose pink and gaudy yellow.
Vivid green stucco palm trees supported the roof, across which wafted Rococo
clouds.

The minarets and cupolas were demolished years ago, but Mossy Hill still
bears their memory, and is now adorned with a similarly incongruous structure:
the Japanese Gateway.

A remnant of the Japan–British Exhibition held in Shepherd's Bush in 1910,
Chokushi-Mon — the Gateway of the Imperial Messenger — appeared in the
Gardens in 1911. It is a facsimile of an old, sacred gateway in Kyoto and made
from Hinoki wood, a lemon-scented cypress cut from a Japanese forest.

Rampant animals, and the legend of a pupil recovering his master's shoe from
a fast-flowing river were carved into the wood by a man called Wada Genyemon.
It took him just 45 days.

In 1936 and 1956, the Gateway was restored by Kumajiro Torii, a woodcarver who settled in Britain after working at the Japan–British Exhibition. His surname means 'gateway' in Japanese.

During the hot summer of 1995 the Gateway was restored again. The roof — previously cedar bark and shingles — was replaced with copper tiles and the surrounding landscape was created. Evoking the natural scenery of Japan, the Gardens of Activity, Peace, and Harmony are places to pause and contemplate. A low, rounded island in the shape of a turtle, and a tall, angular island suggesting a crane rise up from a stream of fine gravel, raked in swirls and ripples and surrounded by soft Japanese plants.

Situated on top of Mossy Mound

63278 KEW GARDENS, THE JAPANESE GATEWAY.

To the south of Cedar Vista, opposite the blackberries

On the right will be seen Chokushi Mon on its mound surrounded by very old cedars.

This beautiful and remarkable structure is worthy of attention because of the perfection of its proportions and for the exquisite delicacy of the carving.

A printed tablet nearby gives a full account of its origin.

The Temple walls are a battlefield, where territory is won with the scratch of a pencil. Silvery marks fight for space in the gloom — scrawled missives, names, bad words. Rude graphite pictures startle ladies with parasols, who turn their heads and pretend not to notice.

Perched at the top of a small hillock amongst sweet-smelling thyme, cistus and lavender, is King William's Temple. It was originally known as the Temple of Military Fame, owing to the cast-iron plaques commemorating various military victories found on the walls inside.

This grand, Doric structure, also known as the Pantheon, was built in 1837 and, according to legend, the mason was cutting William IV's initials into the stonework as church bells tolled for the king's death that summer. The Temple was renamed in his honour.

The building has often been used by visitors as a shelter from sudden downpours; they have stood in the stone room, looking out at the weather as rain dropped from the peaked portico, making the soil smell delicious.

Over the years, some unsavoury individuals have used the Temple for more nefarious purposes. In 1869 Kew's Director Joseph Hooker recommended that it should be enclosed behind a wire fence as some visitors had taken to graffitiing the walls with pencils and cutting the seats with knives.

The Temple's most famous inhabitants are Apollo and Zephyr, two classical marble statues that used to stand under the east roof. Originally shipped to the Gardens from Italy in the late 1700s, they were left in the darkness of their crates until they were discovered in an old shed in 1852 and installed at the Temple. The figures were subsequently restored, during which their fig leaves disintegrated, revealing that the gods' genitals had at some stage been snapped off.

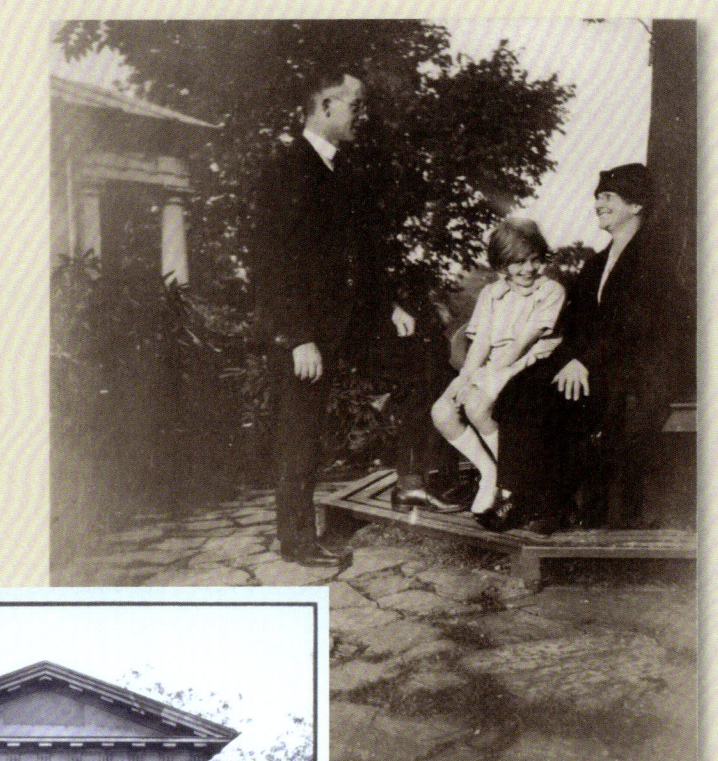

King William's Temple lies amidst heavily scented Mediterranean plants.

Many visitors find it a convenient place to have their picnics on wet days.

Open to the public as a shelter

This temple is between the Palm House and the Temperate House

KYLINS
CHINESE GUARDIAN LIONS

The creatures squat on their great stone
cushions, ready to roll their spheres into
the water. They are ravenous, and lick
the air, glaring down through the cloudy
liquid, scanning the bottom for the flick
of a tail, the promise of firm flesh.

In Chinese mythology a Kylin is a fabulous creature, resembling a lion, thought
to be a good omen foretelling prosperity and luck.

Kew's ten-tonne Kylins are fearsome beasts, with curly manes and pointed
claws. Their powerful paws grip sculpted stone balls, and they crouch at the edge
of the pond, watching the water for signs of trouble, their panting mouths ready
to catch leaping fish.

They arrived at Kew in 1958, but are much older, and believed to date from
at least the 18th century, but could quite possibly have been made in the Ming
period which ended in the mid-1600s.

They are the twins of a bronze pair which live in the grounds of Beijing's
Imperial Palace.

*The steps are flanked by a pair
of magnificent guardian lions*

These statues are situated on the south-east side of the Pond overlooking the water, and are a most imposing addition to the garden ornaments at Kew.

The workmanship is superb

The statues convey an impression of immense muscular strength and vigour and are remarkable examples of the Chinese sculptor's skill in giving vitality to animal forms.

QUEEN'S BEASTS

List of the Queen's Beasts

The creatures in this stone menagerie, installed in front of the Palm House in 1956, are considered to best represent Her Majesty Queen Elizabeth II's royal lineage. The fanciful zoo comprises:

The White Greyhound of Richmond

The Yale of Beaufort

The Red Dragon of Wales

The White Horse of Hanover

The Lion of England

The White Lion of Mortimer

The Unicorn of Scotland

The Griffin of Edward III

The Black Bull of Clarence

The Falcon of the Plantagenets

Winter pounds its frosted fist on the
earth, shivering over the soil, iron-
hardening the water in the Pond. It is
cold — bone-cold, blood-clotting cold.
Icicles decorate the stone zoo — lithe
hearts stopped fast with the twist of a
chisel, frozen by a sculptor's spell.

Ten heraldic figures stare out across the Pond, bearing their pointed teeth and flashing their talons, steadfastly guarding the Palm House.

The lion grins from beneath his regal crown; the white horse clasps an armorial shield tightly between its hooves. The falcon has a terrifyingly sharp-looking beak, and keeps watch with beady eyes over the unicorn, tethered by a chain at his throat. A scaly dragon, black bull, white lion and greyhound with a lolling tongue sit beside two mythical Beasts — the benevolent griffin and the magnificent yale, which, according to mythology, can swivel each of its horns independently.

These fearsome and noble creatures are Portland stone replicas of their plaster cousins — sculpted by James Woodford — which stood outside Westminster Abbey for the coronation of Her Majesty Queen Elizabeth II in 1953.

Three years later, a man called Henry Ross, the wealthy chairman of a Scottish drinks company, paid for the Beasts to be sculpted and installed at Kew. The creatures are said to represent the late Queen's virtuous lineage.

Statues of heraldic figures

Ten royal creatures

The yale is a purely mythical beast whose peculiar characteristic was the ability to swivel each horn independent of the other.

The griffin is one of the most ancient of mythical beasts and despite his formidable appearance was regarded as a beneficent creature.

RUINED ARCH

The weather is a thief, stealing away the
brickwork. Each warm gust snatches at
the terracotta — it crumbles and falls as
powder on the bracken that scrambles
up the earthen bank. Deep shadows are
summer resting places — dark liquid pools,
shelter from the searing day. Merinos move
overhead, sweating in the heat.

Perhaps Kew's truest folly, the Ruined Arch was built in 1759, during the period in which it was popular to construct deliberately ramshackle edifices in the grounds of large country estates, so landowners could be visually reminded of the fragility of humanity.

The design of the folly is based on Roman antiquities, with rusticated encrustations. A triumphal arch mouth and round brickwork eyes stare up and down the pathway beneath.

Deliberately derelict sculpture and fallen masonry are artfully arranged on the ground beneath the Arch, as though an earthquake has just shattered the air and pushed them from their pediments.

During George III's time the folly, perversely, did in fact have a practical purpose — an animal track built over the top provided a way to move sheep and cattle from the King's nearby farm to grazing pastures within the Gardens.

A hundred years or so after the folly appeared in Kew's landscape, two rooms flanking the main archway were opened up, creating the smaller side tunnels which were possibly used as shelters from inclement weather by nightwatchmen patrolling the Gardens.

By 1933 the Arch truly had become a ruin, and reinforced concrete was added to the structure to protect the walls from tree roots which had begun to disturb the brickwork.

In the 1950s the Arch was nearly damaged once more when one of Kew's working horses bolted and cantered through the folly, still dragging its cart, narrowly missing the walls.

THE RUINED ARCH. KEW GARDENS.

A relic of the romanticism of an earlier period

The Arch was designed as a ruin ... at a time when such mock antiquities were fashionable.

It is now much overgrown with ivy and other creepers, which adds to its air of apparent antiquity, and retains a few faked fragments of Roman statuary.

Trailing clematis festoons the sides

Of special interest is the poison ivy ... whose sap causes painful blisters to arise on the skin. It is cultivated in many places ... often where its dangerous properties are unknown, for the sake of its brilliant autumn tints. Many mysterious attacks of skin disease have been caused by men pruning this plant in ignorance of the poisonous nature of its sap.

Some people can handle the plant with impunity while others are afflicted with violent itching from a mere touch of the leaves.

SUNDIAL

Midday. The sun throws a short, stubby
shadow on the dial. Jean Thompson steps up
on the marble pedestal and sets her watch.
That afternoon, her bony, elongated fingers
reach for handfuls of onions, teasing their
shivering skin from the dirt. In the stretched
light, gold shines from the black earth.

In 1832 William IV, son of George III, took one of a pair of sundials casting shadows at Hampton Court Palace and moved it to Kew, depositing it on the lawn in front of Kew Palace, to mark the spot where, over 100 years earlier, an important astronomical observation had been made.

By looking through an enormous telescope, amateur stargazer Samuel Molyneux and his friend James Bradley, Astronomer Royal, discovered the aberration of light, proving that the planet on which they were standing moved around a central, fiery orb. And so, light and time are celebrated in this place, which is perhaps a portal to other moments and spaces.

As the sun made its passage across the sky one day during the Second World War, gardener Jean Thompson was thinning onions growing on the Palace lawn when her fingers stumbled on something hard, buried in the soil — a 17th-century signet ring set with amethyst, on which was engraved a tiny portrait of a woman, staring back at her through time.

The following decade, crusty tobacco pipe bowls and perfect wine bottle seals from a previous century also rose to the surface and were pulled from the loam.

Earlier, in 1916, gardeners watched a Royal Naval air balloon called Swallow fly above Kew before landing close to the sundial, on the spot where the White

House once stood. This former grand residence provided the royal family with additional accommodation to Kew Palace, before it was demolished in 1802. Remains of it were discovered by gardening staff during the First World War when, with their horses, they ploughed the lawn to plant potatoes as part of the national effort.

The sundial ...
stands on the lawn

The spot where Bradley carried
out his astronomical
observations

On this spot, in 1725, the Rev James Bradley made the first observations which led to ... great discoveries.

This dial was placed ... in 1832 by command of His Most Gracious Majesty King William the Fourth.

TEMPLE OF AEOLUS

On blustery days, the seat still squeaks in the wind, crying a thin, melancholy whine that interrupts thought and ruins conversation. Mr Warren has tried his best, but the weather prevails, spinning occupants round the carousel until they are dizzy.

Close to the Temple of Aeolus, on the land now occupied by Museum Number One, another strange folly once stood. The octagonal House of Confucius, built in 1749, cast its mirror into the Pond. The water lapped the bank and rippled, reflecting elegant, latticed windows, bold, Rococo colours and, on the roof, a golden dragon dancing on a ball.

A decade or so later, the Temple of Aeolus was built on the Mound above the Pond. It is named well: after the wind god, who puffs his cheeks and breathes wild breezes over the hilltop, around the pillars holding up the domed roof, and down the wooded slopes, where children used to roll through scratchy grasses as they tumbled towards the water below.

The Temple originally had a revolving seat which provided a circular view of the Gardens. Occupants could turn it to shield themselves from the wind. It was delicate, however, and its repair by Mr Warren, a carpenter, in the late 1700s, was not sufficient and the contraption was eventually removed in 1845.

Today, visitors who climb up to the Temple are rewarded with a wide panorama, from the Kitchen Garden to the Palm House.

Its severely classical lines are particularly effective

Just inside the Cumberland Gate on the summit of the wooded mound is the Temple of Aeolus.

A hill, on which stand some noble trees, and the summit of which is crowned by a little edifice, dignified … with the title of the Temple of Aeolus.

The Mound is artificial in origin, as are all the small hillocks at Kew

TEMPLE OF ARETHUSA

After the ceremony, after the saplings are
pushed into the earth, when the land is
quiet again, a gardener stands in the Temple,
pressing his fingers against the plaque, feeling
the names of his friends. He remembers an
old wood, sunlight silhouetting oak leaves —
a place where tusked boar hunted truffle,
and men hunted each other.

Just like the ancient underground spring that flows beneath this temple, Arethusa, for whom it was named, was, in Greek mythology, a nymph who transformed into a stream that flowed deep under the earth.

This sweet little shelter was built in 1758, but the main focus of its story is rooted in the 20th century. The Temple is a memorial to the 37 Kew staff members who died in the First World War, and 14 more who were killed in the Second World War. Charles, Arthur, Sidney, Harry, Joseph, John, Percy and their colleagues are commemorated on a bronze tablet. These men laid down their gentle trowels and trugs to take up roles in the tank corps, navy, air force and foot police.

The summer after the first war ended, Peace Day, a bank holiday, was celebrated on 19 July. Two young oak trees were planted close to the Temple that day. They were grown from acorns brought back from battlefields of Verdun, France, in 1917.

In 2013, a storm caused so much damage to one of the oak trees that it had to be felled. Timber from the tree was made into a bench, on which people now sit to admire the Temple.

A wreath is laid in the Temple each year on Armistice Day.

The little temple of Arethusa

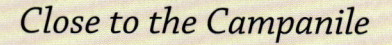

Close to the Campanile

This so-called Temple ... serves to shelter a garden seat above which the names of those Gardens staff who lost their lives in the First and Second World Wars are recorded on a tablet.

Nearby at the end of the pond is a young oak tree grown from an acorn collected in Flanders.

TEMPLE OF BELLONA
TEMPLE OF MINDEN

The royal children look out at the rain,
starfish fingers and squashed noses pressed
against the glass. They watch the Temple
for signs of growth, singing songs about
mushrooms and wishing more buildings
would burst from the damp soil.

The Temple looks so established, up on the rise by Victoria Gate, framed by tall trees that sprinkle their leaves on its domed roof when the wind blows. But it was not always situated here — rather, it was originally erected in 1760 on the land now occupied by the Princess of Wales Conservatory, and transported across the Gardens to its present site in 1802. The royal family, who could see the Temple from the windows of their Palace bedrooms, thought it looked like a mushroom, and called it Mushroom Temple.

The folly is named for Bellona, the Roman goddess of war, who sported a plumed helmet and rode a chariot into battle. The battle it commemorates — Minden — took place in the middle of the Seven Years' War, on the first day of August 1759, the year before the Temple was built.

The room inside is decorated with festoons and medallions celebrating British regiments that fought in the war. Overhead, the blue oval ceiling was painted with a glorious golden sunburst. The Temple is closed to visitors, but at one time provided welcome shelter from both the sun and rain.

During restoration in 1985, the Temple was surprisingly found to be made of wood. Alas this flammable material aided the folly's partial combustion two years later, when fire destroyed some of the roof.

A single rectangular room, covered with an elliptical dome

The walls inside are decorated with stucco festoons and medallions, on which are inscribed the names or numbers of various regiments.

The frieze is carved with alternating helmets and daggers ... the oval dome is painted blue and has in its centre a gilded wooden 'glory' or sun in splendour.

Set on a slight rise to the south of Victoria Gate

The ground in front of the graceful little building is thickly planted with crocuses and just beyond is a group of magnolias ... with ... huge dark pink flowers the size of soup plates.

TEMPLE OF THE SUN

Cracked crimson eggshell scatters across the lawn. Gusts pluck at the frieze of lyres, playing their broken notes. Virgo and Sagittarius turn their eyes skyward, looking up at the heavens they fell from, staring into the heart of the sun.

The Temple of the Sun was built in 1761 on the lawn in front of the Orangery. For over 150 years, visitors made worshipful pilgrimage there, standing in its cool interior and gazing upwards at the zodiac zoo arranged in a bas relief frieze around the central sunburst, gasping at its exquisite scarlet ceiling and pointing at the fish, the bull and the ram, the scorpion, lion, goat and crab.

On a dark March night in the spring of 1916, a storm grabbed at the branches of a great cedar tree growing next to the Temple. Nobody saw it falling, but so it did, smashing the building in one blow, throwing shards of domed roof and Corinthian columns across the grass.

Seven summers later, Queen Mary planted a maidenhair tree on the site in commemoration. In the early 1940s Kew's Director, Arthur William Hill, wanted to replace the Temple with a new model, but government austerity prevented the building of a new stone structure. Instead, a shelter of western red cedar was built in Cambridge Cottage Garden.

Photo Lole & Paddey Ld

*A handsome
architectural
building*

*Richly decorated with lyres,
laurel sprigs, and wreaths of flowers*

We see before us a handsome ornamental building surrounded by a circle of Corinthian columns, and known as the Temple of the Sun.

The shining white Temple of the Sun, destroyed in 1916 by a Lebanon cedar which fell on it during a storm.

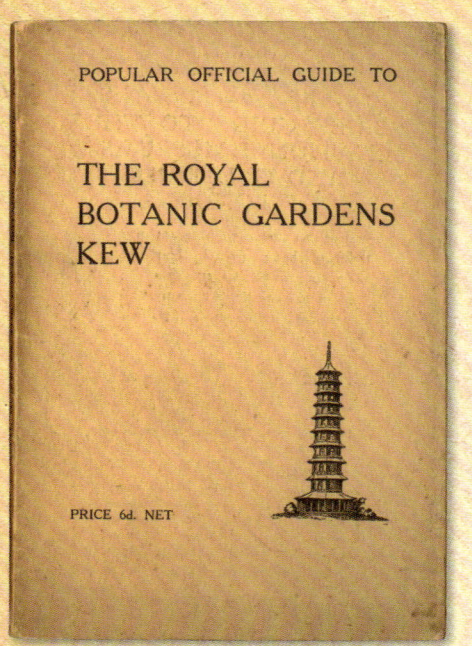

Guidebook from 1938 showing
an image of the Great Pagoda.

Author S. Goldney's unofficial guidebook from the
early 1900s showing a view of the Great Pagoda.

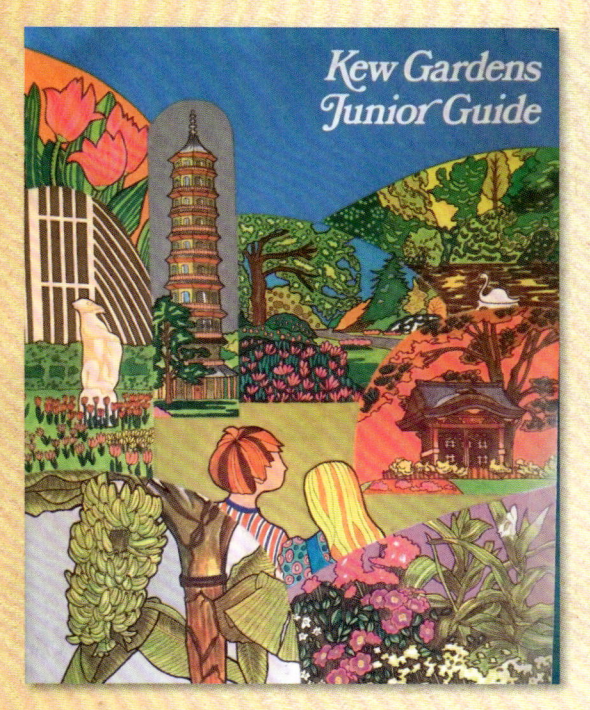

1977 *Junior Guide* showing the Palm House with
one of the Queen's Beasts and the Parterre, the
Great Pagoda, Lake, and Japanese Gateway.

1970 guidebook showing Syon vista.

TREASURE

To people with imagination museums are not just dry-as-dust places full of meaningless things in glass cases, particularly when ... arranged as cleverly as Kew's museums

To complement the plants and flowers growing in the Gardens, Kew has in its storehouses a vast assortment of objects made from their dead and dried remains. The official term for the study of these things is "Economic Botany", but far better is Director William Hooker's description of them in the 1858 guidebook: "curious Vegetable Products".

The first of four museums providing visitors with the opportunity for a close examination of these objects was established in 1848 in the building overlooking the Aquatic Garden, now home to the School of Horticulture. It was the first of its kind in the world.

It was a time when most commodities were made from plants, and thus knowledge and understanding of them was of great importance. The limits of this are described in the 1938 guidebook: "The Museums show us how little, as well as how much, we know of the extent to which herbs, shrubs and trees contribute to our necessities, comforts, and numberless requirements."

The Museum rapidly became incredibly popular — visitors, it seemed, were just as eager as Kew's scientists to discover more about the trees from which their walking canes were made, and the origin of the mint in the comfits they sucked as they stared into the cases.

As the Museum garnered increasing public attention, consequently well-meaning individuals quickly sent a great number of plant products to Kew for inclusion in the collections. Soon the Museum was groaning with trinkets. As a result, in the spring of 1857, Kew opened a new, purpose-built, three-storey Museum across the water from the Palm House. This edifice — considered incredibly ugly at the time — became Museum Number One (the General Museum) and the first Museum was relegated to Museum Number Two (the Reference Museum).

Later, Museum Number Three (the Timber Museum) and Museum Number Four (the British Forestry Museum) were opened in the Orangery and Cambridge Cottage respectively.

A detailed guidebook for each of the four Museums was produced, however. As explained in the 1930 edition, Kew again understood and accepted the limits of its knowledge and sought suggestions from visitors as to how to improve the information it provided for them:

The Guides are not intended to supplant a system of copious instructional labelling, which is being constantly improved upon, and printed labels substituted for those written by hand. Any suggestion bearing upon these, or hints respecting our deficiencies, those who have the charge of this important branch of the Kew establishment will be most happy to receive. Such should be addressed in writing to the Keeper of the Museums, or to the Director of the Royal Gardens.

Although all four museum buildings still stand at Kew, the collections — amounting to some 100,000 objects — now reside in a tomblike underground repository, hidden deep within the undergrowth, and visitors are typically only able to access them online.

However, the doors to another incredible Kew treasure house are still very much open, and a journey over the threshold should not be eschewed. The Marianne North Gallery opened in June 1882 and an incredibly comprehensive "Descriptive Catalogue" detailing the 832 paintings of "Plants and Their Homes" on display was published in the same year.

The Gallery is testament to the adventurousness and artistry of the incredible woman who gave her name, funds and hundreds of paintings to the extraordinary space which holds, as described in the 1951 guidebook: "the life work of that remarkable Victorian, Miss Marianne North". Over one hundred years after the Gallery opened, the experience of visiting had not diminished — as explained in the 1987 guidebook, "the whole effect is breath-taking".

MARIANNE NORTH GALLERY
NORTH GALLERY

Marianne North slams her studio door,
rattling the brushes in their pot. Returning
to the Gallery a moment later, she scratches
the outline of tea and coffee plants on to
the wooden panelling — all the while
growling about her friend.

Painter and adventurer Marianne North returned from travelling around the world in 1879. No sooner had she unpacked her trunk, she picked up her pen and wrote to her friend Joseph Hooker, Kew's Director, asking if she could bequeath to the Gardens her immodest collection of paintings, and pay for a gallery to display them. Hooker, of course, agreed, and the Gallery opened three summers later. The journey to opening, however, proved to be more challenging than some of North's global expeditions.

Knowing from personal experience that rest between excursions is important, North conceived of her Gallery as a place where tired visitors could pause and contemplate, before continuing their day exploring the Gardens. She wanted Gallery visitors to be able to buy, at a fair price, tea, coffee and biscuits, but Hooker refused. Much vexed, North painted tea and coffee plants on a door panel inside the Gallery, to remind the Director of his snub.

Fitting the paintings on to the Gallery walls was difficult too. North took charge of hanging all 832 pictures herself, arranging them in geographical groups around the room and working from a small studio at the rear of the Gallery to produce made-to-measure drawings to fill any awkward gaps in the mosaic she was creating. The space between the ceiling and the floor hummed and sang: Chilean monkey puzzle trees, Brazilian oranges, a wide, clear river flowing through Jamaica, a South African ostrich farm, Egyptian date palms growing by the Nile — all glowing and moving in one vibrant mass of colour and energy.

Finally, in 1882, the Gallery opened — an attractive red-brick building inspired by the grand houses North had seen in India. Although visitors could not enjoy refreshments there, they could shelter on the ornate iron veranda, as could the custodian employed to look after wet umbrellas. The veranda seats were eventually stolen away to the Temperate House, where elderly visitors would snooze on them in the afternoons.

This is the sight no visitor should miss

Whatever else at Kew be done or left undone, the stranger must be pointed to ... the North Gallery ... The pretty building itself will at once invite attention.

Nowhere else, perhaps, can the untraveled person gain so vivid an idea of the scenery and characteristic vegetation of the countries which Miss North visited. Of each country there is a long series of pictures, not only of individual plants and flowers, but of the forests, mountains, rivers, and waterfalls as well. Often the people, their temples and dwellings, are portrayed, and occasionally insect and animal life.

The unique collection of paintings … is together with the Gallery in which it is
placed, a free gift to the Royal Gardens on the part of the accomplished lady-
artist and traveller whose name the Gallery bears. The pictures were painted by
herself, on the spot, in the countries indicated; and were arranged by herself in
the positions which they occupy; and both the preparation and printing of the
catalogue are due to her munificence.

The paintings were so numerous that it was necessary to hang them close together,
and cover the walls from the dado to the cornice, involving months of labour in
adjusting, reducing, painting odd bits here and there, putting in little accessories,
touching up, and finishing off generally.

Some of Marianne North's paintings

The following paintings are amongst those wonderfully described in the original Gallery guidebook of 1882.

Landscape at Morro Velho, Brazil

In the foreground is a colony of butterflies … going to roost on a single segment of a palm leaf, from which they will never move until the sun's rays reach them in the morning. This insect has a powerful musk-like scent by which the artist often found her way to it.

Great Cotton Tree, Jamaica

The silky cotton enveloping the seeds is used to stuff beds and pillows, and hummingbirds line their nests with it.

Flowers of Jasmine Mango or Frangipani, Brazil

Flowers come before the leaves, and when the latter appear a large caterpillar also often comes and eats them all up.

Coconut Palms on the coast near Galle, Ceylon

Dead leaves are tied to the trunks of the Coconut Palm in Ceylon to tell by their rustling when thieves are climbing over them.

Foliage, Flowers, and Fruit of an African Tree painted in India

The flowers open only at night: and this was painted by candle-light.

Antics of Ants among the Flowers

When painting these Proteas ... the artist was not a little surprised to see the florets rising and wriggling and dancing about in a most unaccountable manner, and on investigating the cause of these movements, discovered it to be ants pushing the florets out to make room for their nests.

A Swamp Plant and Moorhen, Seychelles

The Moorhen is remarkable for its very large feet.

Study of Olives, painted in Italy

It has been cultivated in the countries bordering the Mediterranean from time immemorial, and the oil obtained from the fruit is there an important article of food, besides being extensively used in cooking other articles, whilst in this country it is only eaten with salads, preserved sardines, and such things.

The Avocado or Alligator Pear

Those strangers do at first relish the fruit, it is highly esteemed, especially in the West Indies and America, where it usually eaten as a savoury with pepper and salt. It has a firm yellow pulp, possessing a nut-like taste; hence it has been called Midshipman's Butter.

Collection of Fruits, painted at Lisbon

Unfamiliar to most English people is the long purple Aubergine or Eggplant.

Leaf and Inflorescence of a Gigantic Aroid, Java

When it opens it exhales an offensive odour that is quite overpowering, and so much resembles that of carrion.

Leaf-Insects and Stick-Insects

The singular forms assumed by these insects have suggested the names leaf-insect, stick-insect, &c., and these names are most appropriate, for the insects so closely resemble the twigs and leaves of the plants on which they live, that they seem to form part of them. These adaptations, or resemblances between the insects and the plants they feed on, serve to guard the insects against extermination by their enemies.

Possum up a Gum Tree

The pretty little animal was pulled out of a hole in the tree, and a few hours afterwards he had become so tame that he took milk out of a teaspoon.

West-Australia Sand-loving Plants

The soil in this district is so very sandy that, with the exception of a few big stones, the whole country might be run through an hour-glass.

MUSEUM NUMBER ONE
GENERAL MUSEUM

Decimus Burton stops outside the Palm House
to admire his handsome reflection, winking
from the window. He turns on his heel, looks
out across the Pond, and opens his sketchbook.
The paper is strong and square, and the lines
the architect draws upon it are just the same —
he imagines a grand building, a place to store
treasure, a new mark on the land.

Museum Number One was designed by Decimus Burton, the same man whose architectural vision resulted in the stately Palm House. The Museum took two years to build, and was completed in 1857.

That year, one bright May morning, the Curator rattled his newly cut key in the lock, and flung back the double doors of Museum Number One, admitting visitors to this fresh, ochre-coloured building for the first time. They climbed the grand staircase, beginning their journey through the collections from the top downwards, as the special guidebook directed, peering into the glazed mahogany cases with a reverence and reserve at exhibits of maple wood, cashew nuts, fenugreek, red cedar, fish berries, governor's plum, drift fruits and foxgloves, learning how the stems of those pink mittens are sometimes made into sunshade handles.

They goggled at roses made of wax, a wreath of dried blue waterlilies taken from the coffin of Pharaoh Rameses II, and gramophone needles made from prickly pear spines, then paused to rest on benches made of padauk wood, Indian laurel, and camphor wood from Borneo, running their fingers over the polished seats and staring back at the portraits of botanical luminaries who gazed down at them from heavy, gilded frames.

Whilst the permanent collections barely changed over the course of the Museum's history, special exhibitions were staged frequently to provide a series of new reasons for visitors to step inside the building. In 1962, exhibits included a display of live British wild plants and a selection of autumn foliage. The following winter, witch hazel, viburnum, larch and wintersweet clipped from the frosted landscape outside were shown together with photographs of the Gardens in summer, in an attempt to provide artistic contrast. In 1968 the winter display comprised the botanical ingredients of a Christmas pudding.

Museum No.1 is situated between the Cumberland and Victoria Gates, facing the Palm House, and consists of a building on three floors.

*Ample storehouse
of knowledge*

Here we may see in various states, tea, coffee, cocoa, wine, tobacco, hops, nutmegs,
cloves and other more or less familiar friends, with some not so well known in Britain.

Here is the original form of vanilla, made from the fruit of an orchid. Here are
jumping beans from Mexico; henna used by women of the ancient world to stain their
fingernails and the palms of their hands ... Juice used to make deadly the blow-pipe
dart ... a collection of Victorian wax fruit and flowers so true to life that it is difficult
to tell they are not real.

This building also contains portraits and busts of many distinguished botanists.

Some of the exhibits found in Museum Number One

Several editions of the Museum Number One guidebook contain excellent accounts of the objects visitors could find in the cases:

Mango
The fruits are used in India in large quantities for making chutney and for dessert, and consignments of the choice eating fruits may occasionally be seen in the markets of Covent Garden.

Avocado
The Avocado Pear can be used as a salad, alone or mixed with vegetables; it is cooked in various ways, often as a vegetable, whilst the best flavoured forms are used for dessert.

Aubergine
These fruits are sometimes seen in the markets of the British Isles, but they are not in general use in this country, although the plant is often grown for decorative purposes. The fruits are highly esteemed in the countries of the Mediterranean region.

Grape-fruit
Its great use is as an appetiser eaten before or as the first course of a meal, usually breakfast, whilst it is also recommended for its tonic properties and as a specific for dyspepsia.

Holly
It has long been cultivated for the sake of its handsome, evergreen, spiny foliage and its cheerful red berries … At Christmas-tide a large business is done in the sale of berried holly for purposes of decoration.

Willow
The wood is light and tough, and is used for various purposes, such as the bottoms of carts, rims of sieves, polo balls, trug baskets … and the manufacture of first-class cricket bats.

Teak
It is widely used in ship-building, railway work, house, wharf, and bridge building, piles and many other kinds of work where strength and durability are essential … The stairs in this building are made of teak.

Over a hundred cases are here laid out for inspection.

Ebony

Excellent wood for carving, and is also employed for cabinet work, walking sticks, piano keys, turnery, parts of mathematical instruments, chess men, and various other kinds of work.

Coffee

As a beverage, coffee is less popular in the British Isles than in many European countries, the United States of America, or S. Africa ... Caffeine is the addictive principle in coffee.

Peanut

Great care is exercised in the preparation of a high-grade peanut butter. Nuts of different varieties may be blended to obtain just the desired flavour. Roasting and grinding require careful attention. In grinding, the right degree of fineness must be achieved; if too fine the butter clings to the roof of the mouth; if it is too coarse it is gritty.

Brazil Nut

In windy weather collectors may refrain from going near the trees for if one of the hard woody fruits weighing 3 to 4 lbs. and falling from a height of 100 feet should strike the head of a collector the dire consequences may well be imagined.

Almond

They are quite wholesome and those with thin shells are usually used ... for dessert. Others, with thicker shells, are ... sold for use in confectionery. Large quantities are used in the chocolate trade.

MUSEUM NUMBER TWO
REFERENCE MUSEUM

He shuffles up to the window, cupping his
hand against the pane to make a blinker.
Slowly, his old gardener's eyes adjust to the
dim room inside, where cases filled with
strange objects stand in the space which
was once his kitchen, where he cooked
drop scones for his wife, making the whole
house smell of honey and hot butter.

When George III lived in Kew Palace, gardeners grew fruit and vegetables in the old kitchen garden for the royal family to eat. Every autumn, apples were picked from the orchard trees, packed, and carefully stored over the winter in the building which eventually became Museum Number Two.

After it ceased being employed as a fruit store, the building was used as a mess room and packing room, before finally being made into a modest, ivy-cloaked home for a senior gardener, until one day in 1846, when Kew's first Director, William Hooker, arranged objects from his personal collection of 'vegetable products' on a groaning trestle table, displaying them proudly for government commissioners who he persuaded to allow him to make the building into a museum. When it opened two years later, it was the first of its kind in the world.

A gallery was fitted at first floor level, and a skylight cut into the roof. A carpenter installed glazed cabinets to the walls and table cases were placed in the large, central room.

Quickly, the building became a hoarder's paradise, stacked from floor to ceiling with curious objects from around the world. Woven shrimp baskets, fans and a hammock dangled from the rafters; the corridors were crammed with specimens — fish nets made from palm stalks, creepers, hats, tablemats and beehives, fruits preserved in bottles of spirit.

In 1857 Museum Number One was opened opposite the Palm House, and much of the collection was moved into this larger home. Since 1990 the building that was once Museum Number Two has been Kew's School of Horticulture; today students learn about living plants in the same room that housed so many of their dead ancestors.

A depositary for all kinds of useful and curious Vegetable Products

One had but to see the crowds frequenting in summer the existing Museum
(so great that the Director finds it frequently impossible to enter at public hours
with distinguished visitors, who desire to have objects explained to them), to be
satisfied of the deep interest the public take in such a collection ... It has done more
to recommend and popularise ... the science that communicates a knowledge of the
vegetable creation, than all the princely palms, the gorgeous waterlilies, the elegant
ferns ... which grace the tropical houses of these noble Gardens.

Filled with specimens of dried fruits and seeds

The general arrangement of the collection has proved instructive; and the marked attention of many visitors, the notes that are taken in the room, and the works of artists performed there, show that it is so.

The utility of this Museum to mankind at large, and of that arrangement of the collection which we have been discussing, is testified by the remark of not a few visitors, "Now we see for the first time in our lives, and on a large scale, a practical application of the science of Botany."

So valuable and extensive a collection required a cheap and popular guidebook similar in size and plan to that for the Gardens; and the present has consequently been published.

MUSEUM NUMBER THREE

TIMBER MUSEUM (ORANGERY)

The trees on the lawn turn away from the
building, bowing their heavy branches
and crying leaves on to the damp grass.
Inside, slain comrades have been chopped,
turned and sanded. The sickly smell of
furniture polish pervades the huge room
— a mausoleum, filled with elegant chairs,
sturdy doors and carved wooden frames.

In 1862 the International Exhibition, a world's fair, was held in London's South Kensington on the site now occupied by the Natural History Museum and Science Museum. Thousands of objects from 36 different countries were on display, showcasing the very best of manufactured, crafted and raw materials. Afterwards, one of the exhibits — a magnificent collection of timbers and woods — was given to Kew and put on view in Museum Number Three, the Timber Museum, in the Orangery.

Subsequently, timbers from other international exhibitions including those held in Vienna, Paris, Philadelphia and St Louis were also added to the Museum collection.

Specimens on display in the Museum included hundreds of wooden walking sticks and an immense sketch of an aroid which was pasted to the ceiling. In the 1940s, the beautiful, fungal drawings of Kew's chief mycologist and President of the British Mycological Society, Elsie Wakefield, were exhibited in the Museum.

In 1883 spiral staircases twirling upwards to a new first floor gallery were added to the building, to give the exhibits and their visitors more room.

In 1959 Kew decided to transform the Orangery back into a citrus house and so the Museum contents were transferred to Museum Number Four, the British Forestry Museum, in Cambridge Cottage.

Museum No. III, or the old Orangery ... situated at the north end of the Broad Walk near the Publication Kiosk.

Many examples of woodcraft

Trees and wood are a source of great interest and pleasure to a great many people on account of their aesthetic and their economic value. The great size and great age that some trees attain is remarkable.

The natural beauty of woods and the great diversity of grain ... that exists is well exemplified in the special exhibit of veneers used for panelling and interior decoration.

*Devoted chiefly
to specimens
of timber*

In front of the end window ...
is a well-preserved specimen
of a totem pole ... also the
hollowed trunk of an elm
used as a water pipe ... An
interesting exhibit illustrating
the manufacture of toy
wooden animals ... occupies a
case in the centre of the room,
and on the other side the
method of making violins is
illustrated. A table case near
the entrance ... contains an
interesting collection of woods
used for making walking sticks
and umbrella handles.

MUSEUM NUMBER FOUR
BRITISH FORESTRY MUSEUM
WOOD MUSEUM
(CAMBRIDGE COTTAGE)

The slice of tree is bigger than the boy.
He crouches beside it, using his fingers to
count the rings, working outwards from the
ancient heart, whispering numbers under his
breath. The tree is older than him, older than
his mother and father. Nearly as old as
a dinosaur. Nearly as old as a star.

Grandson of George III, the Duke of Cambridge lived in his eponymous Cottage until his death in 1904.

The Duke and his family liked to take breakfast and tea in the Garden Room. Other rooms in the house included the Drawing Room, Dining Room, Library and a room for billiards. Fashionable parties for fashionable people were held on the lawn.

Six years after the Duke's demise from a stomach haemorrhage, Kew opened his former home as the Museum of British Forestry, and filled it with native timbers, gruesome-looking equipment used for toppling them, and information about the diseases that plagued them. In one of the three upper rooms, a display of injurious animals, insects and fungi included information and photographs showing deer and squirrels feeding on tree bark, rabbits nibbling on saplings, and a collection of knobbly galls.

A great slice of redwood was rolled in; visitors would count its 1,335 growth rings. Forester's hooks, saws and axes flashed fiercely from the cases. One wall was adorned with two pencil drawings — sketched by an Archdeacon — of a large horse chestnut which once stood by the river near the Rhododendron Dell. The room above the entrance hall was stuffed with sports equipment made from British trees — cricket bats of white willow, hockey sticks and tennis rackets made from ash, beech croquet balls.

In 1957 the Museum became the Wood Museum. Today, it can be hired as a venue for weddings and other functions, and many couples have been married in the Duke's old house.

*The collections
are intended
to illustrate
British Forestry*

Museum IV is devoted to British forestry and, by means of specimens of timbers, pictures, photographs and models, as well as by examples of implements, tools, articles in domestic use and wood-ware generally, illustrates the growth of timber in the British Isles and the various uses to which it may be put. A printed guide may be purchased inside the building that gives a full account of the exhibits.

Standing erect like sentinels at the entrance to Museum No. IV are two large tree trunks ... In these two trees is symbolised the purpose of the museum which is to demonstrate the size and quality of timber that may be grown in Britain from native and foreign trees in our woodlands and parks.

On passing into the entrance hall it will be noticed that the walls are lined with some magnificent planks ... a vista of planks of all sizes and kinds meets the eye, representing nearly every kind of tree that can be grown in the British Isles. It is a rare feast to the eyes of a timber enthusiast. He may study the colour and texture of the wood, the ripple and curl of the grain and compare one kind with another to his heart's content.

ROYAL BOTANIC GARDENS, KEW

OFFICIAL GUIDE TO THE MUSEUMS OF ECONOMIC BOTANY

No. I
Dicotyledons

Fourth Edition, Revised and Augmented

LONDON :
SOLD AT THE ROYAL BOTANIC GARDENS, KEW

Printed for His Majesty's Stationery Office by
Wyman & Sons, Ltd., Fetter Lane, London, E.C.4.
1930

Price 2s. 0d. Net

70–55–1.

1930 guidebook to Museum Number One. At the time, the collections in Museum Number One and Museum Number Two were divided respectively into Dicotyledons — plants that have a pair of embryonic leaves on either side of the stem — and monocotyledons, which have one embryonic leaf.

ROYAL BOTANIC GARDENS, KEW.

OFFICIAL GUIDE

TO THE

MUSEUMS OF ECONOMIC BOTANY.

No. 4.

BRITISH FORESTRY.

LONDON:
SOLD AT THE ROYAL BOTANIC GARDENS, KEW,
Printed by HIS MAJESTY'S STATIONERY OFFICE.

1919.
Price 1s. net.

1919 guidebook for Museum Number Four.

POPULAR OFFICIAL GUIDE TO

THE ROYAL BOTANIC GARDENS KEW

PRICE 6d. NET

BOOK TWO

....

HOW TO VISIT KEW

TRANSPORT & PARKING

For a long time, the only way to reach Kew was by riverboat. Royalty and their courtiers would be skulled in skiffs and wherries downstream from Windsor Castle and Hampton Court Palace, or upstream from filthy, sweaty London to their handsome riverside retreat on the banks of the Thames.

According to guidebook writer Robert Hope Moncrieff, author of the unofficial *Kew Gardens* (published in 1908), by the time Kew opened to visitors in 1841, they could be ferried to the Gardens by "steamboats plying in the summer time up the devious reaches of the river".

By the mid-1800s, the railway had arrived at Kew, with stations at Kew Bridge and in Kew Village; horse-drawn trolley-buses also ran past the Gardens, up and down Kew Road.

As naturalist Philip Gosse explains in his unofficial guidebook, *Wanderings through the Conservatories at Kew* (published in 1856), visitors hoping to reach Kew for a day's recreation were spoilt for transport options:

> As to conveyance, there are railroads for those who have little time, the omnibus for those who have more, and the steamboat, taking the chances of the tide, for those who have most. Whichever route we adopt, the way thither is a pleasant one, and we are sure of what the pent-up Londoner gasps vainly after — free and fresh air, and plenty of breathing-room.

As well as relying on public transport visitors could, of course, use their own means to make their way to the Gardens. William Dallimore, who spent his working life looking after Kew's Arboretum, recalled the variety of vehicles arriving at Elizabeth Gate (then the Main Gate) on busy Sundays at the end of the 1800s: "Four-horse coaches and brakes, pair and single-horse broughams, phaetons, wagonettes, ralli cars, dog-carts, gigs, horse-cabs, hansom cabs, costers' carts drawn by ponies or donkeys".

23421 Kew. Road & Entrance to Gardens.

Many of these vehicles needed places to stop or idle, but at the time there was no official parking place, and so they clogged Kew Green. Indeed, it would be a number of years before the Brentford Car Park opened by the riverside, and then only in peak season, as explained in the 1959 guidebook: "Queen Elizabeth's Lawn, now used as a car park, is manned from just before Easter till the end of the summer only."

The car parking lawn was named after Elizabeth I because she was supposed to have once sat beneath an old elm tree which grew there. The tree was eventually blown down and subsequently made into a kitchen table for Osborne House, the royal residence on the Isle of Wight.

Before Kew created a place for visitors to park motor vehicles, in 1900 a cycle shelter was installed close to Elizabeth Gate where velocipedes could be left in the charge of a former gatekeeper named Nixon for twopence each. That year 6,326 cycles were deposited in the shelter in the space of six months.

Whether by road, rail, river, or other means, as guidebook writer Robert Hope Moncrieff explained in 1908, "from all parts of London it is easy to get to Kew", and over centuries, visitors have followed various well-travelled routes to make their own pilgrimage to the Gardens.

38921 Kew Pier.

Botanic Gardens
KEW
CYCLE SHELTER

No. 543

G. ⚜ R.

ROYAL BOTANIC GARDENS, KEW.

Cycle Shelter.

CYCLE DEPOSITED.

To be given to Owner.

SEE CONDITIONS ON BACK.

PK142
No. 543

G. ⚜ R.

ROYAL BOTANIC GARDENS, KEW.

Cycle Shelter.

To be affixed to Cycle.

Cycles are received only on the express condition that the Board of Agriculture and Fisheries shall not be liable for the loss, misdelivery, or detention thereof, or damage thereto, unless occasioned by the wilful misconduct of the Board's Servants. All Cycles not claimed within half an hour after closing time will be detained until next day, and must be reclaimed at the Office, 197, KEW ROAD. A charge of One Shilling per night for each Cycle so detained will be made.

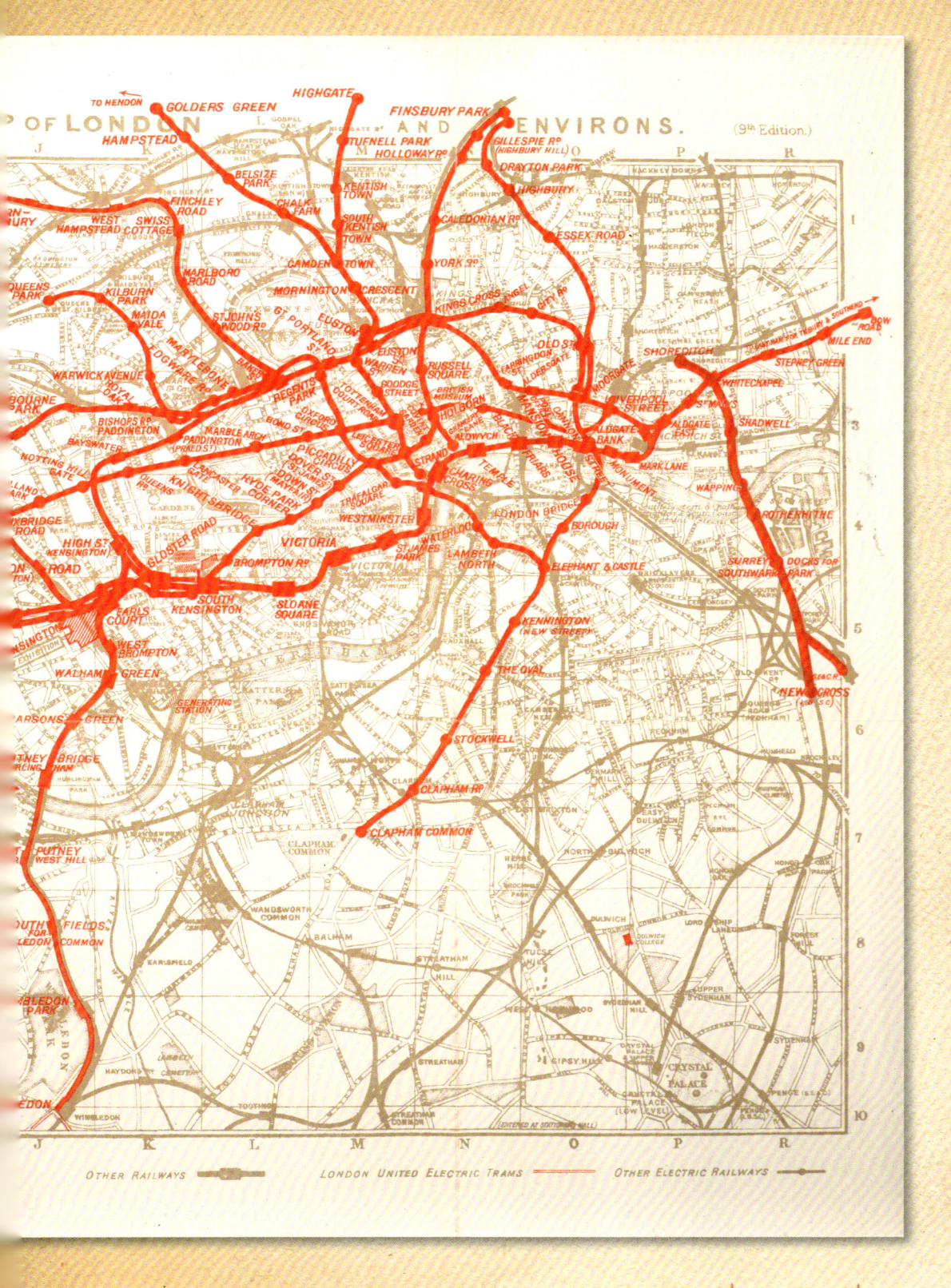

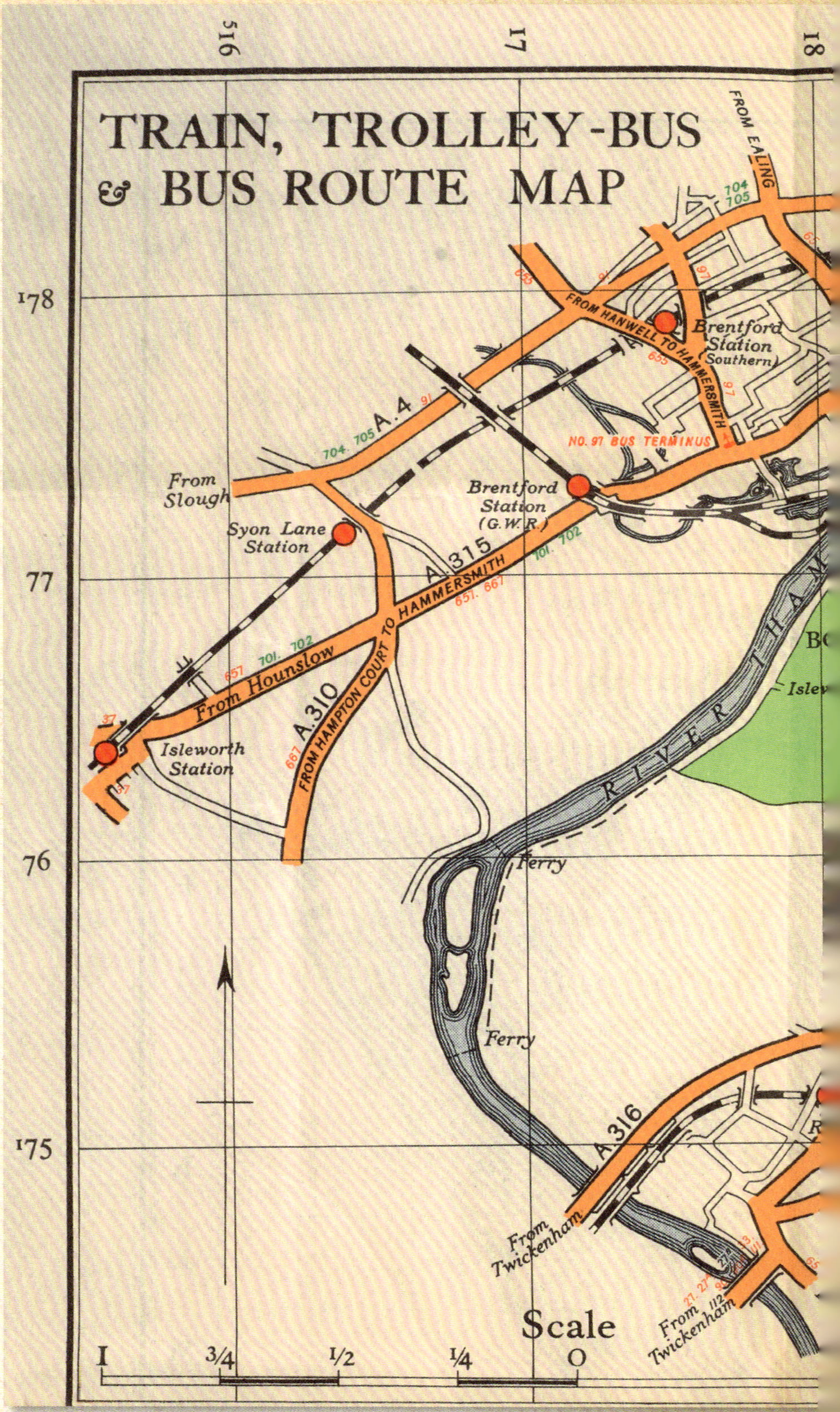

TRAIN, TROLLEY-BUS & BUS ROUTE MAP

516 17 18

178

77

76

175

From Slough

Syon Lane Station

704 705 A.4

A.315

From Hounslow

A.310 *FROM HAMPTON COURT TO HAMMERSMITH*

657 701 702

651 667

101 702

Isleworth Station

Brentford Station (G.W.R)

Brentford Station (Southern)

NO. 97 BUS TERMINUS

FROM HANWELL TO HAMMERSMITH

FROM EALING

704 705

Ferry

Ferry

RIVER THAM

Islew

Bo

A.316

From Twickenham

From Twickenham

R

Scale

I 3/4 1/2 1/4 O

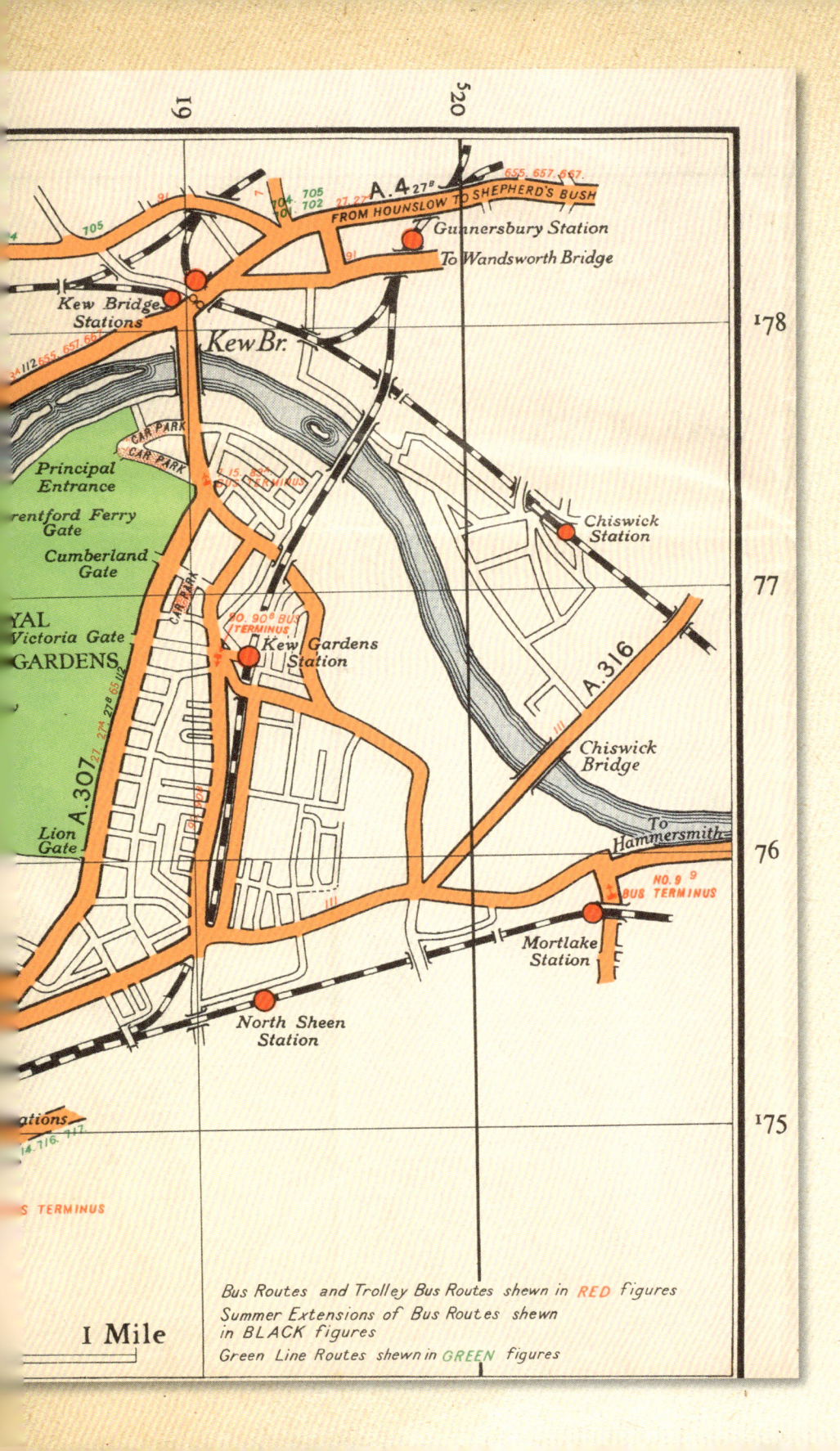

Bus Routes and Trolley Bus Routes shewn in RED figures
Summer Extensions of Bus Routes shewn in BLACK figures
Green Line Routes shewn in GREEN figures

1 Mile

GATES
PUBLIC ENTRANCES

List of gates

Kew's 300-acre landscape can be accessed via a number of openings cut into the brick boundary wall that snakes round the perimeter of the Gardens. Today only four public gates are in use, but previously, many more have opened and closed:

Brentford (Ferry) Gate

Cumberland Gate

Elizabeth Gate / Main Gate / Principal Entrance

Herbarium Gate

Isleworth (Ferry) Gate

Jodrell Gate

King's Steps / Stair Gate

Lion Gate

Lower Nursery Gate

Nash Gate

Oxenhouse Gate

Princess Gate

Shaft Yard Gate

Unicorn Gate

Victoria Gate / Queen's Gate

For the majority of the 1900s, visitors could enter the Gardens by six different gates. As detailed in the 1930 guidebook, "besides the Main Entrance on Kew Green, the Gardens have five other public entrances: three on Kew Road, viz., the Cumberland, Victoria, and Lion Gates; and two on the side of the River Thames, the Brentford and Isleworth Ferry Gates".

Many of the guidebooks from this period are in fact arranged in sections corresponding to the gate by which visitors might enter, as explained in the 1930 guidebook: "It will be for the convenience of visitors to point out and review briefly the various objects of interest which are in the neighbourhood of the respective entrances, or are most conveniently reached from them."

Several of the guidebooks feature walking tours, plotted on a map, taking visitors on interesting circuits of the Gardens and delivering them back to whichever of the six gates from whence they entered. These six gates are celebrated here.

Opened in 1846, Kew's oldest extant public gate is Elizabeth Gate, also known as the Main Gate or Principal Entrance. Its grandeur is best described in the 1858 guidebook: "On approaching the Botanic Gardens by the ... entrance at the head of Kew Green, the visitor cannot fail to be struck with the beauty of the richly ornamented gateway."

When installed, this gate was a physical representation of the sea-change in Kew's attitude towards its visitors. No longer were they required to scuttle apologetically through a small doorway cut in the wall and be escorted everywhere they went by crabby gardeners with untrusting eyes; now they were welcomed through an ornate portal decorated with a noble coat of arms and foliage flourishes. As naturalist Philip Gosse extolled in his unofficial 1856 guidebook, "the beautiful iron gates open and usher us into the exquisitely-kept grounds".

The Gate was originally flanked by two lodges, atop which sat a Coade stone lion and unicorn. These beasts now guard the Lion and Unicorn Gates which open on to Kew Road.

Victoria Gate, as suggested in the 1912 guidebook, is a "convenient starting point" for visitors wishing to make the most of their day at Kew, and, as explained in the 1930 edition, was "chiefly used by visitors who arrive by railway at Kew Gardens Station". The same is true today, with the majority of Kew's visitors now using this gate to enter the Gardens.

Indeed, this gate was specifically built to accommodate visitors arriving at the new station in Kew Village. Originally called the Queen's Gate for the monarch it is now named after, the gate was installed in 1868 in a hole punched in the wall opposite the Temperate House. The route between the station and the gate would have been a short, straight line. However, when the station eventually opened it was — annoyingly — located a third of a mile further north. Consequently, the gate was taken down, renamed, and opened in its current spot in May 1889.

Sometimes, Lion Gate is known as Pagoda Gate, for this is the landmark which visitors first encounter when passing into the Gardens through this entrance. As explained in the 1930 guidebook, the Gate is "situated at the south-east corner of the Gardens nearest Richmond, from which it is easily reached by omnibus". Lion Gate Lodge, the architecturally elaborate house sited next to the Gate, was built in 1863 for a Kew foreman.

One of two riverside entrances to Kew, Brentford (Ferry) Gate was — as explained in the 1930 guidebook — "used by visitors who reach it by ferry across the Thames" and was "chiefly convenient for pedestrians on the towing path who wish to enter the Gardens, or those inside who desire to reach the riverside". However, a riverbank jaunt at that time cannot have been as pleasant as it sounds: Brentford factories belched forth smoke from coal-fired furnaces, and the waterside was terribly polluted.

Further upstream, in the south-west corner of the Gardens, close to the end of Syon Vista, lay Isleworth (Ferry) Gate, on the Thames riverbank. It opened in 1872, and at that time was no more than a wooden drawbridge lowered during Kew's opening times to allow visitors to trip trap over the haha which separates the Gardens from the towing path. The Isleworth Ferry operating here commuted visitors across the river until the late 1970s.

The last of Kew's six 20th-century entrances is Cumberland Gate which was, as explained in the 1930 guidebook, "the first one on the Kew Road passed by omnibuses coming from the direction of London". It opened on to a "pretty and informal scene": Cumberland Mound, on which the charming Temple of Aeolus is perched. This gate closed in 1996 — by then it was not used frequently enough to justify the cost of keeping it open.

Kew's gates tell the story of the Gardens' popularity over time, of its attitudes to public access, and the importance with which the organisation views itself, reflected in the gates' grandeur. Millions of visitors over hundreds of years have stepped over these thresholds, beginning and ending their adventures in the Gardens.

OPENING TIMES

During Joseph Hooker's directorship of Kew in the mid-1800s, he was repeatedly harangued by groups of prospective visitors who wished to be able to access the Gardens at all hours of the day and night. At first Hooker remained reticent in the face of their demands and thoroughly inflexible in his attitude towards opening hours. If it had been up to him, the Gardens would not have opened to the public at all.

Gradually however, he capitulated, at least in part, agreeing to open a few parts of the Gardens for a limited number of hours on some days of each week. It was not until the 1900s that the public was given a much freer choice regarding when they could visit Kew — commencing on New Year's Day 1921, Kew opened daily (except Christmas Day), in both the mornings and afternoons, allowing visitors to wander freely about the landscape as they pleased.

Yet how Kew's 20th-century visitors were able to keep track of which times the Gardens were open or closed, is anyone's guess. The guidebooks make it clear that Kew's management seemed (probably inadvertently) intent on confusing visitors by presenting constantly changing opening and closing times.

In 1951, the guidebook stated that the closing hour varied "from 4pm in midwinter to 8pm in midsummer", yet failed to specify precisely during which of those four hours the gates might shut, leaving visitors to risk being locked in for the night. By 1987 Kew opened at 9.30am, but the closing hour again varied, "from 4pm–6.30pm on weekdays and 4pm–8pm on Sundays and Public Holidays, depending on the time of sunset".

Even more bewildering were the opening times of the various glasshouses and museums — Ernest Law's unofficial guidebook, *Kew Palace Illustrated — A Popular Guide To The Palace And Its Contents With A Catalogue Of The Pictures* (published in 1925) states that the building was open on "Sundays, Mondays, Wednesdays, Thursdays and Saturdays, 1 to 6 in summer; 1 to 4 in winter" and

on "Tuesdays and Fridays, 10 to 6 in summer; 10 to 4 in winter". The 1959 guidebook stated that "the Houses and Museums are open daily from 1pm; they close ten minutes before closing time during the winter but are never open after 4.50pm on a weekday or 5.50pm on a Sunday". The Alpine House followed its own rules, and was only open "in the mornings from 10am to mid-day and 1pm to closing time", presumably to afford the gardening staff a lunch break.

Today the Gardens are more accessible than ever — both early-morning opening and late-night events are widely promoted.

ADMISSION

Until 1916, entry to the Gardens was free. However in January of that year, as a contribution to the First World War effort, Kew introduced the incredibly reasonable admission fee of a penny, which raised nearly four thousand pounds in the inaugural year. Despite being imposed for a good cause, the charge was met with some opposition, as the Gardens were a popular resort for impoverished East End Londoners and the new admission fee prohibited many of them from continuing to visit. Consequently, the Labour government abolished the charge when they came to power in 1924, but it was imposed again in 1926 by the Conservatives. A second Labour government removed the charge once more in 1929, only for the Tories to reinstate it in 1931.

After this initial political flip-flopping, Kew's penny admission remained in place for another twenty years, disregarding inflation, and became legendary. During that time, millions of visitors took coins from cloth pockets and warm palms, pushing them into the slot in the Gardens' famous turnstiles. Writing in an unofficial guidebook, *The Romance of Kew — Where Flowers Always Bloom* (published in 1950), author Nowell Hall describes the value for money that Kew provided: "For the nominal sum of one penny, the visitor can enter the Gardens, there to find out how interesting and prolific nature can be when wisely assisted by the expert gardener."

On April Fool's Day 1951 Kew increased the admission charge to threepence, and there it remained until the advent of decimalisation two decades later, when Kew chose the nearest whole equivalent of three old pence as the new entry fee: one new penny. However, as one new penny was actually equal to 2.4 old pence, the entry fee had in fact decreased.

The next price hike appeared in 1980 when the admission charge was raised to 10p, a price equivalent to about 40p today. In the four decades since, Kew's entry fee has slowly increased, reflecting the enhanced visitor offer the Gardens now provide.

As well as standard admission, Kew has sold all manner of different ticket types to its visitors over the centuries, including season tickets, group tickets, tickets for wheelchair users, concessions for older and younger people, permits for visitors who wish to sketch or photograph the Gardens, and chits for perambulators and luggage.

The economy afforded to visitors through their purchase of annual season tickets made them a popular option. As explained in the 1979 guidebook they could be obtained "on application to the Director or from the Orangery Bookstall at a charge of £1.08" but — somewhat fiercely — adds that they "may be revoked at the discretion of the Ministry of Agriculture, Fisheries & Food", the government department responsible for the Gardens at the time.

By the mid-1900s Kew was issuing special tickets for visitors who wished to use wheelchairs (then described as invalid chairs) and pushchairs (perambulators) in the Gardens. Unfortunately however, the Kew landscape was not entirely accessible at the time, as explained in the 1951 guidebook: "invalid chairs and perambulators must not be taken on the lawns, nor into any buildings". From the 1960s, wheelchairs could also be hired from Kew, as the 1967 guidebook details: "a limited number are available for hire at a charge of one shilling for three hours. It is advisable to notify the Director in advance of requirements."

As explained by writer Robert Hope Moncrieff in his unofficial guidebook published in 1908, "the pictorial or landscape aspect at Kew attracts a large and increasing body of painters, photographers, and picture-makers for the whole of the spring and summer months". Keen to capitalise on this, Kew issued special "photographic apparatus" tickets from 1916 onwards, at a cost of threepence. In 1920, over 3,000 of these camera tickets were sold. By the mid-1900s artistic activity was permitted freely in the Gardens but, as decreed in the 1961 guidebook: "Sketching and photography in the houses are allowed by permit only on the afternoons of Fridays. Applications for such permits should be made to the Director." Imagine

the handwritten requests to sketch Kew's trees and flowers stacked on the Director's desk, as he busily authorised permits for long Friday afternoons when visitors carrying palettes laden with vermillion and cadmium painted Kew, with licence, onto their canvasses.

Although the number of total annual visitors admitted to Kew has been recorded since entrance figures began to be kept in 1841, they are considered to be wildly unreliable and therefore broadly meaningless, although a general upward trend in the years since admission was first charged in 1916 can be observed. A member of the Kew Constabulary, recalling bank holidays in the 1950s remembered "days when you literally couldn't move on the Broad Walk and we used to get streams of people coming in off the Thames boats". Certainly, contemporaneous photographs of the Gardens show them to be remarkably crowded with pleasure-seekers who all happily swapped a few pence for a memorable day out.

GUIDEBOOKS

Once through the gates visitors unfamiliar with Kew have, since 1847, been able to purchase a guidebook in order to understand the immense, labyrinthine landscape. As explained in the 1858 edition, "strangers, or persons not well acquainted with the vicinity of Kew, often entertain very incorrect notions of this establishment; nor can such be wondered at ... taking into account its extensive and highly-varied nature".

Whilst it is true that one of the many delights to be had at Kew is the sense of surprise, of encountering the unexpected around each corner, a deeper knowledge of the Gardens can also much enhance visitors' understanding. By using a guidebook whilst walking the land, information about various features can be gleaned and digested — it can take a lifetime to know Kew, and a guidebook can certainly help expedite that learning.

Over the years, guidebooks have been able to be bought from the bookstall or publications kiosk, the gates, the various shops, and even through the post. Guidebook prices have of course increased, but are generally relatively inexpensive: sixpence in 1912; two shillings and sixpence in 1967; £1.25 in 1986.

Alas, in the early 1940s, guidebooks were in short supply as a warehouse containing government stationery caught alight after being hit by a wartime incendiary. The remaining stock was incredibly slight, and was stored in the Director's office for safekeeping until a reprint could be arranged.

Writing in the *Journal* of the Kew Guild, Kew staff member Hazel Hyde recalled her role at Kew in the mid-1960s: "Every Thursday afternoon we used to have to go on our rounds with a barrow-load of guidebooks, making sure all the gates had a good supply for the weekend."

Many of the guidebooks suggest routes around the Gardens for visitors to follow, taking in various features of particular interest, as explained in the 1970 edition: "This guide is arranged in the form of a circular tour of the Gardens, starting at the Main Gates, and proceeding clockwise." This approach follows a long-standing Kew tradition — even before Kew was a public Garden, in the second half of the 18th century the monarchy and their guests would follow a designated route or "royal circuit" around the landscape, that would lead them from the Orangery to the Temple of the Sun and Great Stove, past the Temples of Bellona and Aeolus to the Ruined Arch, the Alhambra, the Great Pagoda, Mosque, Gothic Cathedral, and finally to the Temple of Solitude.

The proposed routes recommended in the guidebooks were clearly too much for some, however, and in 1985 one visitor decided to abandon directions given on the inside of the guidebook altogether, and focus instead on the front cover. After her visit she wrote to Kew's Enquiry Unit, enclosing an invoice for shoe repairs and claiming that her footwear had been worn out wandering the paths of Kew all day as she sought the aerial view of the Temperate House she had seen on the front cover of her guidebook.

List of rules

Kew's rules feature in almost all its guidebooks. The 1858 edition contains a long and detailed list of edicts that visitors had to obey, or face the severe consequence of being summarily ejected from the Gardens and not invited back.

1. *Smoking, or eating and drinking, or the carrying of provisions of any kind into the Gardens, are strictly forbidden. No dogs can be admitted.*

2. *No packages or parcels, bags or baskets, are allowed to be carried within the grounds. All such articles must be deposited at the gate of entrance while the owners make the tour of the Gardens.*

3. *No person attired otherwise than respectably can enter, nor children too young to take care of themselves, unless a parent or suitable guardian be with them: the police have strict orders to remove such, as also persons guilty of any kind of impropriety. Nor can large schools have admission, except in accordance with the printed regulations to be seen at the gate.*

4. *It is by no means forbidden to walk upon the lawns; still it is requested that preference be given to the gravel-paths, and especially that the lawn-edges parallel to the walks be not made a kind of footway, for nothing renders them more unsightly. It might scarcely be thought needful to say, that all play, leaping over the beds, and running, particularly on the mounds and slopes, are prohibited; yet the latter has been practiced, and so heedlessly, that very serious injuries have resulted from falls, and grievously scarred faces have been the memento of such folly. The Gardens are intended for agreeable recreation and instruction, not for idle sports.*

5. *It is requested that visitors will abstain from touching the plants and flowers: a contrary practice can only lead to the suspicion, perhaps unfounded, that their object is to abstract a flower or a cutting, when detected, must be followed by disgraceful expulsion.*

6. *It is particularly requested that visitors will enter the plant-houses by the doors indicated for the purpose; if they do otherwise, and come in by opposite ones indiscriminately, they will meet and pass each other, which the narrowness of the walks renders difficult; and this must occasion inconvenience to all parties, and often injury to the plants. The accompanying Plan of the Gardens and plant-houses will, it is expected, prove useful; and a stranger to the ground and the collection may do well to follow the route indicated by dotted lines, as the most convenient for giving a tolerably complete survey of the whole.*

In the interests of protecting its precious plants and buildings, Kew has long sought to carefully control and confine the behaviour of its visitors. In order to achieve this, rules, or Statutory Regulations "to be observed by persons using the Gardens at Kew" have been displayed at the gates for centuries.

These Regulations still apply to visitors today, and together with some more mundane rules about opening times, guide dogs and children, they feature some very Kew-specific orders, including not to worry birds or take their eggs, skate on the ornamental water, or smoke a lighted pipe in the plant houses. Using "profane, indecent or obscene language" and being "clothed in a manner reasonably likely to offend against public decency" are also forbidden, as is lighting fireworks.

Visitors prone to misbehaving can reasonably be apprehended by a member of the Kew Constabulary, an extant security force established in 1845 comprising Metropolitan policemen, and, from the mid-1850s, army pensioners who had fought in the Crimean War. For years they have patrolled the Gardens, on the lookout for visitors committing crimes and misdemeanours, and, it transpires, their presence has not been unwarranted — in 1881 a visitor called Miss Stone was caught whacking the flowers off a rhododendron bush with her parasol.

When reprimanded by a constable, she spitefully snapped off a large branch from the bush, to further demonstrate how the plant mattered naught to her.

As explained in the 1858 guidebook, however, most of Kew's visitors rarely abused the privilege of being admitted to Kew, and William Hooker, Director, writing in the preface to that edition, bore "willing testimony to the excellent conduct of the many thousands who frequent the Gardens". Notwithstanding this, Kew continued to post directions at the gates concerning how visitors were expected to behave whilst in the Gardens, and also featured lists of rules in almost all its guidebooks, whilst also retaining the belief that rules should not really be required, as explained in the 1935 edition:

> Except for a few regulations absolutely necessary in a public garden visited frequently by great crowds, the intention is that visitors should enjoy the place with as little restraint as they would in their own gardens. Is it too much to ask of them, the real owners of this great national possession, that in return they should do their best to preserve the amenities of the place?

One common Kew crime was the theft of plants — a little light propagation carried out by visitors for their own benefit. It is easy to suppose that they were so overcome by the horticultural excellence and the splendour of the flowers and blossom that they wanted to take that beauty home with them.

THEFT OF SPECIMENS

WARNING is hereby given that legal action will be taken against any unauthorised person who takes away or plucks any flower, plant or other exhibit.

The Gardens Constables have power to inspect the contents of bags, baskets or other receptacles in cases of reasonable suspicion.

(Authority : The Parks Regulation Acts, 1872 and 1927 ; The Royal Botanic Gardens, Kew, Regulations, 1927.)

Other guidebook edicts encouraged visitors not to climb trees, not to throw orange peel or paper on the ground, and, in the 1980s, not to play "radios and cassette players".

However, in contravention of its otherwise constricting code of conduct, it has always been permissible to walk on the grass in the Gardens, as detailed in the 1935 guidebook: "The attention of visitors is drawn to the fact that no restrictions with regard to the use of the lawns exist at Kew", and for years visitors have revelled in kicking off their sandals on hot summer days and feeling the turf between their toes.

EATING & DRINKING
REFRESHMENTS

When intrepid painter Marianne North sponsored the Gallery at Kew in which she hung her hundreds of paintings, she beseeched Director Joseph Hooker to include provision within the building for the serving of tea and coffee, but, despite much imploring on North's part, Hooker seemed immune to her entreaties.

A visionary in more than one regard, North's wish to offer refreshments to tired, thirsty visitors was eventually realised — not in her Gallery, but not too far away. Kew's Refreshment Pavilion opened on the first day of August 1888. Romantically described by writer Robert Hope Moncrieff in his unofficial guidebook published in 1908, its location was: "beyond the Palm House in an open glade".

The Pavilion's first menu included the "Shilling Tea", comprising freshly made tea or coffee, homemade bread and butter with preserves, cake, and, in a cursory nod to health, salad. According to the season, visitors could enjoy fowl and ham, galantine of chicken, and cold salmon; for one shilling and sixpence, the meaty "Cold Collation" was also available, featuring various cuts from a farmyard of slain animals: ham, tongue, beef (roast, pressed or boiled), and veal and ham pie. Whilst the movement of other vehicles in the Gardens was restricted, the butcher's boy was permitted to cycle through the landscape in order to deliver his fleshy parcels to the Pavilion.

Alas, all this feasting came to an abrupt end one cold February morning in 1913, when Arboretum foreman Arthur Osborn, who lived in a dwelling at the bottom of the Gardens, was awoken at about quarter past three in the morning by a loud crackling noise. Rising and drawing back his bedroom curtains, he saw flames engulfing the Pavilion. Upon reaching the building moments later, he found it impossible to operate the fire hose hanging on the side of the building due to the ferocity of the flames, and so ran to Lion Gate to call the fire brigade.

They arrived within half an hour, but it was too late — the wooden nature of the building and a strong north-easterly breeze made it impossible to save. It was later discovered that the fire was deliberately set by suffragettes Olive Wharry and Lillian Lenton.

The new Pavilion opened in October 1915, with an expanded menu. Drinks included tea, coffee, cocoa, chocolate, milk, draft lemonade, ginger beer, lemon squash and Bovril, and visitors could also be tempted by buns, sponge cake, madeira cake, genoa cake, cherry cake, French pastries, Swiss roll and a compote of fruits, rolls served with butter and greengage jam, as well as ices and strawberries and cream in season.

By the mid-1900s, as explained in the 1959 guidebook, as well as providing table service for "food and drinks as set meals" the Pavilion had also adopted the modern "cafeteria system", which was clearly very popular — by 1976 the eatery could easily serve 3,000 visitors on a busy Sunday, although the consequent challenges of litter and scavenging bird attacks were not uncommon.

Unfathomable now from a commercial perspective, but perhaps in an attempt to counteract overcrowding at the Pavilion, many of Kew's 20th-century guidebooks suggest alternative dining options outside the Gardens, for example

the 1951 edition, which proposes that visitors try the "several restaurants on Kew Green, and others close to the Cumberland and Victoria Gates".

In order to provide further eating opportunities within the Garden walls, Kew opened a Tea Bar in the spring of 1965, which, as explained in the 1970 guidebook, could "easily be reached from both the Brentford Ferry Gate and the Main Gate [Elizabeth Gate]". The edible plants growing around the new café included olive trees and delicious-looking berries.

By the late 1980s Kew recognised that the Pavilion and the Tea Bar alone were no longer enough to sustain the hungry hordes of visitors, and so also opened a café in the Orangery, serving, according to a visitor leaflet, "cold carvery lunches and afternoon tea … with finger sandwiches and fancy cakes" as well as melon cocktail, a smoked salmon mousse and "exotic salads".

Around the same time, the Kew Bakery, close to Kew Palace, offered takeaway pizza for picnics in the Gardens; however this eatery was destroyed in a fire in the 1990s.

Today, Kew's refreshment offer includes the Pavilion, Orangery and a café at Victoria Gate, as well as the Botanical Brasserie, where visitors can dine in the building which was previously Museum Number One, the General Museum, sipping hot beverages in the place where tea, coffee and cocoa plant specimens were once displayed.

The Refreshment Pavilion. Kew Gardens.

The Tea Gardens, Kew Gardens

Naturally, as the number of visitors to Kew increased in the 1840s, so too did the need to provide them with specific toilet facilities, in order that they did not use the landscape as a latrine.

A charming "cloakroom" (which still exists today), at the Orangery end of the Broad Walk, close to Kew Palace, is described in the 1858 guidebook. Here, women could "always find a place of rest or shelter in wet weather … where their umbrellas or cloaks can be deposited by those who contemplate a long walk, under the care of an obliging female attendant". In 1932 this facility was doubled in size and separate exit doors were added in order to help visitor flow.

In the same year, the "lavatory accommodation for gentlemen" at the back of Museum Number Three, the Timber Museum, was modernised. Three years later, men were prioritised again, with more loos added for them near the Ruined Arch, which included "washing facilities", and by the mid-1900s Kew had updated all visitor toilets by installing within them automatic turnstiles.

At that time, however, there was a disparity between the number of toilets provided for each gender, with only four ladies' loos, but six for men, as the 1951 guidebook sets out:

Lavatories – For Ladies: (1) near Museum III, (2) east of the Lily Pond, (3) east of the Tea Pavilion, (4) east of the pond. For Gentlemen: (1) behind Museum III, (2) near Brentford Gate, (3) east of Tea Pavilion, (4) just south of Cumberland Gate, (5) near Victoria Gate, (6) east of the Lily Pond.

It is interesting to note, also, that toilets for men and women were, for the most part, in different parts of the Gardens, rather than being available in the same block, as they are today.

TOURS
GUIDE LECTURER SERVICE

For most Kew visitors, a guidebook is sufficient an aid to facilitate their navigation of the landscape. Others, however, prefer to lean on the services of a living, breathing, talking guidebook: a tour guide (or, as several of the guidebooks describe this service: "guide lecturer").

Kew's inaugural tours took place in April 1913, originally costing two shillings and sixpence for morning tours, and one shilling for tours which took place in the afternoon. These charges were subsequently reduced in 1914 to sixpence and threepence respectively. According to the tours leaflet from that time, visitors had to sign their names in a book before the tour commenced, and a constable was in attendance "to collect fees and to prevent unauthorised persons attaching themselves to the party".

In return for their fee, visitors were led around the Gardens, plant houses and museums, where objects of particular botanical interest were pointed out by Mr S. T. Dunn, the official tour guide, of whom one impressed visitor wrote the following endorsement:

The most delightful thing to do
In summer is to visit Kew.
No garden can with it compare.
Have you an afternoon to spare?
At 3 o'clock you should be there.

For threepence only they provide
In Mr. Dunn a perfect guide.
If you know much, he'll tell you more;
If you're a dunce, he'll open the door
Of botany and woodland lore.

A dozen visits are too few
To taste the full delights of Kew
For underneath the summer sun
No guide deserves the mark A1
More thoroughly than Mr. Dunn.

Despite this glowing testimonial, on the whole Kew's tours were not particularly popular with visitors, and ceased in 1920.

However, by 1960 Kew was again providing tours for its visitors and appointed a new guide lecturer that year. Kew's tour guides had doubled in number by the following decade — as explained in the 1979 guidebook, "two guide lecturers are available to take parties ... around the Gardens, glasshouses and museums" and that should visitors wish to take advantage of this offer they should "make an application in writing to the Secretary not less than a week before the date of the proposed visit". Clearly these tours were more successful than the experimental versions of earlier in the century; by 1987 the guidebook instructed visitors interested in taking a tour that "early booking is necessary to avoid disappointment".

In the 1990s walking tours were much in demand, and visitors were spoilt for choice, with many different guided walks being provided, including the

"Rainforest" tour, a unique introduction to the wonders of tropical jungles; "Life began in the sea", which took parties into the bowels of the Palm House to look at the Marine Display; and "Cinderella of the Arboretum", which focused on "one of the less well-known glasshouses at Kew" — the Temperate House.

In 1999 Kew introduced the Explorer, a land-train which tows visitors through the landscape. Tour guide drivers deliver an interesting and spirited commentary, pumped through a loudhailer.

Today, as well as being able to experience a tour of the Gardens onboard the Explorer, visitors can also enjoy a more intimate, tour guide-led introductory circuit of Kew on almost every day of the year.

SHOPPING

Almost as soon as Kew began to properly welcome visitors in 1841, it realised the consequent retail opportunity presented by the sudden influx of a receptive crowd, who, without wishing to contravene the strict rules regarding plant theft, wanted to possess a piece of the Gardens.

Souvenir guidebooks were one of the first retail items to be sold at Kew, beginning with first Director William Hooker's *Kew Gardens Or, A Popular Guide to the Royal Botanic Gardens of Kew*, published in 1847, which was quickly snatched up by eager visitors keen to know more about the landscape they were experiencing. By the end of the century, maps and separate guides to the Museums could also be purchased in the Gardens.

To meet visitors' fervent clamour for souvenirs, in 1924 a special Publications Kiosk was opened next to the Orangery. Here, as well as guidebooks, postcards depicting attractive Kew scenes could be purchased. As explained in the 1935 guidebook, "a large selection of postcards in black and white and in natural colours" were available and could be bought either as single cards for a penny,

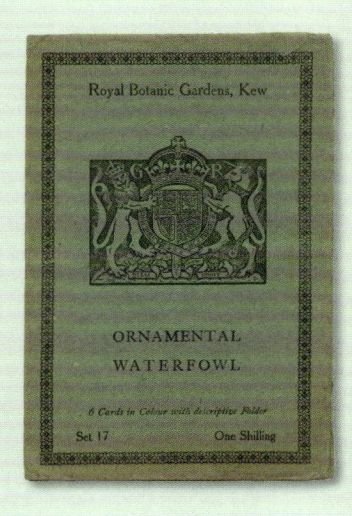

or as sets in a "descriptive folder" with coloured cards costing twice as much as monochrome versions. In addition to providing goods at the Kiosk, Kew also offered a prototype mail-order service, allowing visitors to write to the Curator in order to obtain their postcards by post.

Maps were very popular with visitors who were unfamiliar with Kew's terrain. In 1935 they were able to purchase a *Key Plan of the Gardens* which was, as the guidebook for that year promotes, handily "lined off in squares". The map was sold at three pence, or for two shillings and nine pence the "de luxe" version was available. By the mid-1900s, an Ordnance Survey map of Kew could also be purchased in the Gardens.

In the 1970s the Kiosk was known as the Bookstall, and by that time sold much more than books, as detailed in the 1970 guidebook, "The Bookstall faces the Broad Walk, by the west side of the Orangery. In it, postcards and transparencies, guide books and maps of the Gardens can be bought, as well as other publications."

Not content with the limited shopping space afforded to visitors by the Bookstall, by the following decade Kew's retail team had annexed the Orangery itself, maximising on the 1980s commercial boom by expanding the Kew range

to include gifts, greetings cards and other souvenirs, such as "The Kew Crystal Collection" — special crystal-cut wine glasses engraved with a palm tree motif; and limited edition collectors' plates made from fine bone china and rimmed with 22-carat gold. As a contemporary advert promoting the Orangery shop declared: "a visit to Kew is not complete without calling into the Orangery, whether to buy or browse".

Kew took shopping seriously in the 1990s — as well as generating vital revenue, the Head of Retail described it as something that could "make or break the visitor's impression of Kew". In 1992, the shop moved from the Orangery to the new Visitor Centre at Victoria Gate. Bestsellers included soaps, pencils, mugs, and a new "Eau de Kew" fragrance collection featuring spray, bath gel and pot pourri, with aromas of spicy clove, thyme, rosemary, mint and sandalwood. Kew also harnessed telephone and video technology, operating a "tele-ordering" service and releasing *A Journey Through Kew* — a new official video guide featuring "the entrancing landscapes of Kew Gardens and their many intriguing architectural gems ... using rare archival material and breath-taking aerial footage", which visitors could purchase on video cassette for just £14.99, taking a souvenir of the Gardens home with them.

Fold-out map published in 1946 showing Mosque Hill at the site of the Japanese Gateway.

1903 map with instructions on how to use it.

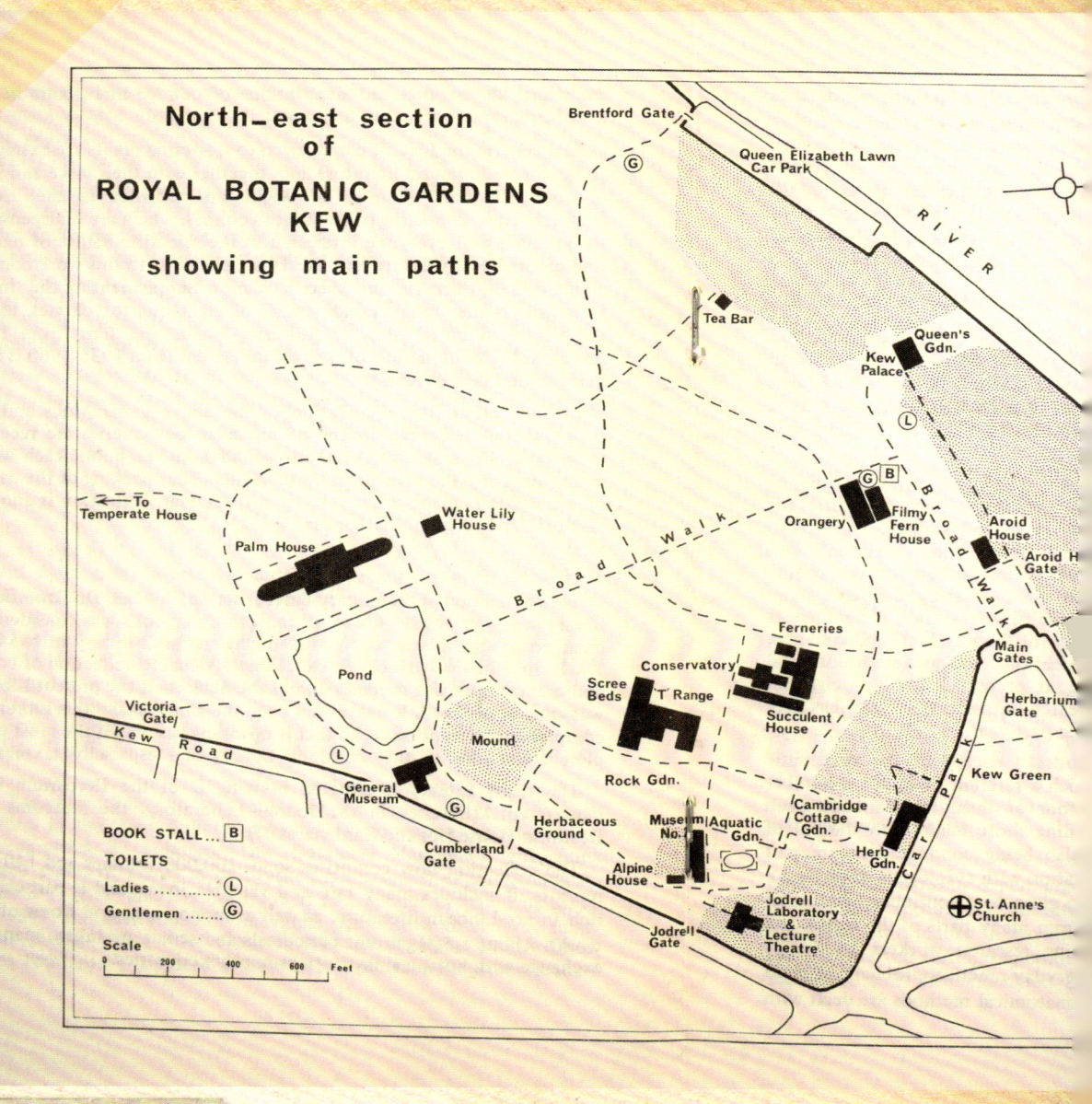

1971 map showing the north-eastern section of the Gardens and main paths.

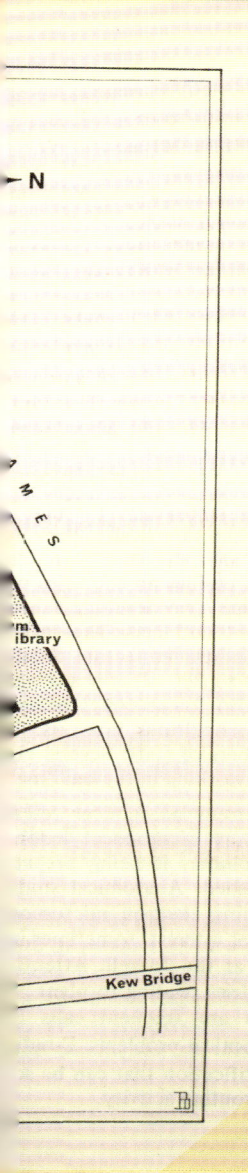

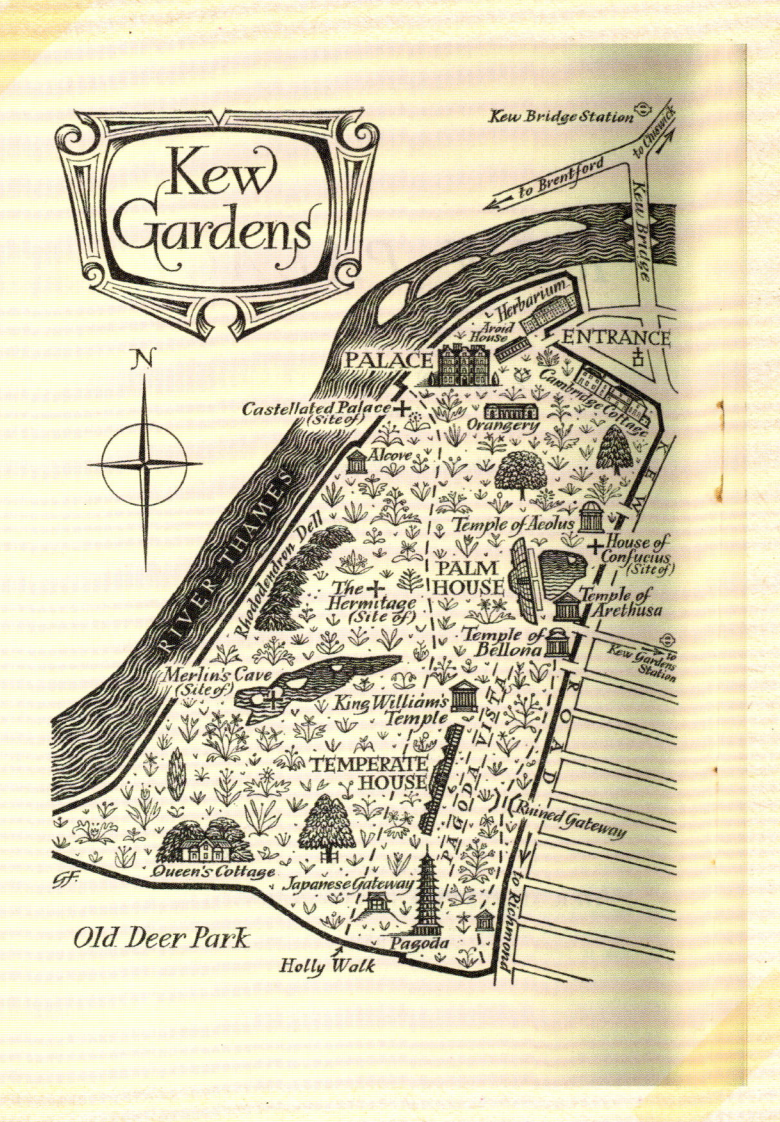

Pictorial map from author John Charlton's unofficial guidebook *Kew Palace*, published in 1956.

1911 French map showing the River Thames and the "Grand Lac".

JARDINS DE KEW

HOUSE

Brentford

Les Water-Closets sont désignés par les lettres: h Hommes d Dames

4-11 Imp. Dufrénoy. Paris.

Map from the 1986 guidebook. The Princess of Wales Conservatory, which would open the following year, is shown as the "Tropical Conservatory".

Royal Botanic Gardens Kew

Guides, Picture Postcards and Publications may be purchased at the Shop F 16

Scale of Metres

300   400   500   600

Area of Gardens approximately 120 hectares (300 acres)

...sed in Winter   τ Public Telephone   R Invalid Ramp

NOTE: To find any object of interest, look for the name in the index, and opposite to it observe the letter and figure (marked thus for Japanese Gateway J3). Then look down either side of the plan for the black letter and along the top or bottom for the black figure, and the object will be found in the square where the lines cross.

If we have half an hour to spare before sunset, we may wander through the groves and avenues, enjoying the delightful coolness of an English summer's evening — not the less pleasing by the contrast of its freshness and breezy gales with the hot and teeming atmosphere of some of the tropical houses that we have left. The squirrels are chasing each other over the grassy lawns, so verdant and so neatly shaven, or play at bo-peep among the branches of the pine-trees; blackbirds are seeking worms beneath the shrubs, celebrating their successful researches in mellow notes from the bushy covert; the green woodpecker, with his scarlet cap, is rattling away on yonder ancient hornbeam; and scores of smaller birds are warbling forth their evening carols, preparatory to putting their heads behind their little wings. The hum of the bee falls on the ear as he sails heavily along towards his distant hive, loaded with spoils from yonder beds of mingled blossoms; and the fragrance that floats to us from the same quarter almost tempts us ... to go there, and lie down, and roll, and revel among the sweet flowers, just as the bee has been doing ... Well, we have seen much to admire, much to please our sense of what is lovely and beautiful and graceful; much to move our wonder and instruct our reason; much to excite our thankfulness in seeing how deeply we are indebted for luxuries, comforts, and necessaries, to the vegetable world.

NOTES

Notes on the words and pictures

As you will by now have gathered, a lot of this book comprises wonderful quotes taken from Kew's historical guidebooks. As explained in the Preface, rather than writing a history book, my goal has been to create an impression of Kew throughout time. For this reason I have deliberately chosen to date neither the quotes nor the photographs in this book. Through the portal which is Kew, I want you to be able to dip in and out of time, experiencing the Gardens alongside past visitors from several centuries at once.

When using the guidebook quotes, in the interests of achieving a consistent look and feel across these pages, I have on occasion removed or added a full stop and capital letter here and there, but not so dramatically as to change the meaning or emphasis of the original text. For ease of reading, I have also removed the scientific names of plants and fungi that were sometimes included in the historical guidebook text.

You will, I am sure, have noticed that several of the buildings and landscape features have more than one name — for example, the Aroid House has been known variously as the Tropical Aroid House, the Nash Conservatory, Grecian Conservatory, Architectural Conservatory and Architectural Greenhouse. I have used all the names I found printed in the guidebooks, again so as to present a zoetrope of Kew: a carousel of moving images rather than a static snapshot.

About snapshots — the photographs decorating these pages come from a variety of sources: from the guidebooks themselves, but also from my own collection and from Kew 's incredible archive. I have deliberately tried, where possible, to use pictures showing visitors, in order to support one of the central tenets of this book — the experience of visiting Kew.

It was William Hooker (Director from 1841 to 1865) who essentially created the Kew landscape we know today — commissioning many of the extant buildings and shaping the soil into the patchwork of gardens you can still visit. The earliest guidebooks I have consulted date from Hooker's time, and the latest from the end of the 20th century, therefore representing a period of approximately 150 years, but essentially still broadly reflecting the landscape that Hooker would have known. It is his Kew that this book reveals.

BIBLIOGRAPHY

Conducting research for this book has been almost as enjoyable as writing it. Naturally, I read a great number of guidebooks — most of which were useful, and almost all of which were beautiful. I also indulged in general reading about Kew's history. Many of all these books are either still in print or can be found cheaply enough second-hand. If you, like me, are at all interested in Kew's fascinating past, I would urge you to obtain your own copies and appreciate them as much as I have.

As well as the books listed below, in order to better understand the history of the Gardens I have relied on information contained in historical editions of the *Kew Bulletin* (Kew's official journal), and in the almanacs of the Kew Guild.

Aiton, W., *Hortus Kewensis, Or, A Catalogue Of The Plants Cultivated In The Royal Botanic Garden at Kew*, George Nicol, London, 1789.

Anon. *London And Its Environs, Including Excursions To Brighton, The Isle of Wight, Etc — Handbook For Travellers*, Baedeker, K., Coblenz & Leipsic, 1873.

Anon. *Southern Germany and Austria, Including the Eastern Alps — Handbook for Travellers*, Baedeker, K., Coblenz & Leipsic, 1873.

Bartholomew, J., *The Magic of Kew*, The Herbert Press, London, 1988.

Bean, W., *The Royal Botanic Gardens, Kew — Historical and Descriptive*, 2nd impression, Cassel & Company Ltd, London, 1908.

Bingham, M., *The Making of Kew*, Michael Joseph Ltd, London, 1975.

Blunt, W., *In for a Penny — A Prospect of Kew Gardens: their Flora, Fauna and Falballas*, Hamish Hamilton, London, 1978.

Chambers, W., *Plans, Elevations, Sections, And Perspective Views Of The Gardens And Buildings At Kew In Surry, The Seat Of Her Royal Highness The Princess Dowager Of Wales*, J. Habaerkorn, London, 1763.

Charlton, J., *Kew Palace*, HMSO, London, 1956.

Cloutman, P., *Royal Botanic Gardens, Kew — A Souvenir Guide*, Royal Botanic Gardens, Kew, 2001.

Cope, T., *The Wild Flora of Kew Gardens — A Cumulative Checklist from 1759*, Royal Botanic Gardens, Kew, 2009.

Desmond, R., *The History of the Royal Botanic Gardens, Kew*, 2nd edn, Royal Botanic Gardens, Kew, 2007.

Desmond, R. and Hepper, N., *A Century of Kew Plantsmen — A Celebration of the Kew Guild*, Kew Guild, Kew, 1993.

Goldney, S., *Kew Gardens — A Popular Guide and Souvenir*, Gale and Polden Ltd, London, 1907.

Goldney, S. (ed), *Illustrated Guide To The Royal Gardens, Kew,* Waverly Press, London, undated (1900s).

Gosse, P., *Wanderings through the Conservatories at Kew*, Society for Promoting Christian Knowledge, London, 1856.

Hall, N., *The Romance of Kew — Where Flowers Always Bloom*, Hampton Court Books, Hampton Court, 1950.

Hall, N., *The Romance of Kew — History, Guide, Map and Pictures of the Gardens*, Hampton Court Books, Hampton Court, 1966.

Hand List Of Rock Garden Plants Cultivated In The Royal Botanic Gardens, Kew, 4th edn, HMSO, London, 1934.

Hand List Of Trees And Shrubs Grown In Arboretum: Polypetalae, Part 1 — Royal Botanic Gardens, Kew, HMSO, London, 1894.

Harrison, C., *Kew's Big Trees*, Royal Botanic Gardens, Kew, 2008.

Hemsley, W., *The Gallery Of Marianne North's Paintings Of Plants And Their Homes, Royal Gardens, Kew — Descriptive Catalogue*, Spottiswoode & Co, London, 1882.

Hepper, N., *Royal Botanic Gardens Kew — Gardens for Science & Pleasure*, Her Majesty's Stationery Office, London, 1982.

Hill, J., *Hortus Kewensis*, Richard Baldwin & John Ridley, London, 1769.

Hooker, W., *Kew Gardens — A Popular Guide To The Royal Botanic Gardens of Kew*, 16th edn, Cambridge University Press, Cambridge, 2013 (facsimile of the original text which was published in 1858 by Longman, Brown, Green, Longmans and Roberts, London).

Hooker, W., *Museum of Economic Botany Or A Popular Guide To The Useful And Remarkable Vegetable Products In The Two Museum Buildings Of The Royal Gardens of Kew*, 3rd edn, Cambridge University Press, Cambridge, 2013 (facsimile of the original text which was published in 1858 by Longman, Brown, Green, Longmans and Roberts, London).

Hope Moncrieff, A., *Kew Gardens*, A&C Black, London, 1908.

Jackson, J., *A Year in the Life of Kew Gardens*, Frances Lincoln Ltd, London, 2007.

King, R., *The World of Kew*, Macmillan, London, 1976.

King, R., *Royal Kew*, Constable & Company Ltd, London, 1985.

Kew Gardens — *A Hand-Book (With Plan) For The Guidance Of Visitors To The Royal Botanic Gardens and The Pleasure Grounds And Park*, J. Martin, London, 1887.

Kew Gardens Junior Guide, HMSO, London, 1977.

Kew Palace — Richmond Upon Thames, Department of the Environment, London, 1983.

Law, E., *Kew Palace Illustrated — A Popular Guide To The Palace And Its Contents With A Catalogue Of The Pictures*, Hugh Rees Ltd, London, 1925.

Official Guide To The Royal Botanic Gardens and Aboretum, 29th edn, HMSO, London, 1885.

Oliver, D., *Guide To The Royal Botanic Gardens And Pleasure Grounds, Kew,* 24th edn, HMSO, London, 1867.

Orangery, Royal Botanic Gardens, Kew, HMSO, London, undated (1970s).

Parker, L. and Ross-Jones, K., *The Story of Kew Gardens in Photographs*, Arcturus Publishing Ltd, London, 2013.

Parsons, N., *Worth The Detour — A History of the Guidebook*, Sutton Publishing Ltd, Stroud, 2007.

Paterson, A., *The Gardens at Kew*, Frances Lincoln, London, 2008.

Perrédès, P., *London Botanic Gardens*, Wellcome Chemical Research Laboratories, London, 1906.

Popular Official Guide To The Royal Botanic Gardens Kew, HMSO, London, 1938.

Popular Official Guide To The Royal Botanic Gardens Including An Historic Notice And Descriptions Of The Collections In The Botanic Gardens Proper, The Glass Houses, Museums And Arboretum, HMSO, London, 1912.

Popular Official Guide To The Royal Botanic Gardens Including An Historic Notice And Descriptions Of The Collections In The Botanic Gardens Proper, The Glass Houses, Museums And Arboretum, HMSO, London, 1924.

Price, K., *Kew Guide*, 2nd edn, Royal Botanic Gardens, Kew, 2007.

Princess of Wales Conservatory, HMSO, London, 1987.

Queen's Garden, Royal Botanic Gardens, Kew, HMSO, London, 1969.

Royal Botanic Gardens, Kew — Open Day 1971, Royal Botanic Gardens, Kew, 1971.

Royal Botanic Gardens, Kew — Illustrated Guide, HMSO, London, 1930.

Royal Botanic Gardens, Kew — Illustrated Guide, HMSO, London, 1935.

Royal Botanic Gardens, Kew — Illustrated Guide, HMSO, London, 1951.

Royal Botanic Gardens, Kew — Illustrated Guide, HMSO, London, 1959.

Royal Botanic Gardens, Kew — Illustrated Guide, HMSO, London, 1961.

Royal Botanic Gardens, Kew — Official Guide To The Museums of Economic Botany, No. 1 Dicotyledons, 4th edn, HMSO, London, 1930.

Royal Botanic Gardens, Kew — Official Guide To The Museums of Economic Botany, No. 4 British Forestry, HMSO, London, 1919.

Royal Botanic Gardens Kew — Ornamental Waterfowl, HMSO, London, undated.

Royal Botanic Gardens, Kew — Souvenir Guide, HMSO, London, 1967.

Royal Botanic Gardens, Kew — Souvenir Guide, HMSO, London, 1970.

Royal Botanic Gardens, Kew — Souvenir Guide, HMSO, London, 1979.

Royal Botanic Gardens, Kew — Souvenir Guide, HMSO, London, 1986.

Royal Botanic Gardens, Kew — Souvenir Guide, HMSO, London, 1987.

Shillito, S., *Love From Kew — A Postcard Scrapbook*, Kew Publishing, Royal Botanic Gardens, Kew, 2020.

Simpson, R., *Simpson's Illustrated Guide to Kew Gardens*, Simpson, Richmond, 1892.

Skipwith, P. and Webb, B., *Edward Bawden's Kew Gardens*, V&A Publishing, London, 2014.

Smith, R., *A Year At Kew*, BBC Books, London, 2004.

Turrill, W., *The Royal Botanic Gardens Kew — Past and Present*, Herbert Jenkins, London, 1959.

Wallis, E., *Illustrations of the Royal Botanic Gardens, Kew, from photographs taken by permission*, E. Wilson, London, 1900.

ACKNOWLEDGEMENTS

Making a book is not a singular task, and I am indebted to many others who have laboured alongside me to produce the volume you now hold in your hands.

Firstly, I would like to acknowledge the many unnamed, unknown writers of Kew's historical guidebooks. Without their original words this book would not exist. I hope you have enjoyed their elegant, precise, and often humorous turns of phrase that I have carefully copied on to these pages. In addition, praise should be given to people from the past who took the photographs I have included, not least a man named E. J. Wallis, who, as the 1800s became the 1900s, took the most sensitive photographs of the Gardens I have ever seen.

Huge and heartfelt thanks go to Gina Fullerlove and Lydia White from Kew's Publishing team, who extended to me the faith, patience and encouragement required to write this book. I shall be forever grateful to them both for allowing me to realise my long-held ambition. I would also like to thank Georgina Hills for her excellent production expertise, Kevin Knight for his artistry, Christine Beard for her superb design and seemingly endless patience, Pei Chu for her splendid image research and Paul Little for his image digitisation skills.

Thank you Ellen Reid for winkling out my writing tics and in particular for pointing out that Kew's Kylins sit upon stone cushions; and thank you Matthew Seal for a keen proofreading eye.

Profound gratitude is extended to staff from Kew's Library and Archives team, not least Kiri Ross-Jones, Kat Harrington, Arved Kirschbaum and Craig Brough, who all helped me to find the most astonishing things, hidden away in Kew's proverbial dusty attic.

I would like to thank Elisa Field for telling me about what was (or, more accurately, wasn't) hidden beneath Apollo and Zephyr's fig leaves. Thanks go too to Greg Redwood, for his enjoyable enthusiasm about Kew's history and for helping me to identify some long-demolished glasshouses.

I am honoured that Dr Janina Ramirez has so kindly said such lovely things about my writing.

I am indebted to Katie Read for her enthusiastic promotion of this book.

I am incredibly grateful that, firstly, the Kew Guild exists, and moreover that they have digitised their annual *Journal* and shared it online — I discovered so many fantastic secrets by looking within the covers.

Thank you Toby Fountaine for taking a nice photograph of me.

DB — thank you, as always, for your kindness and your wisdom, and for not once questioning whether rummaging through old guidebooks was more important than addressing a calamity cupboard's worth of shared responsibilities.

ABOUT THE AUTHOR

Sophie Shillito writes about spirit of place, palimpsests, and microhistories. She is the author of two other books: *All The Little Places* is a haunting poetic-prose tapestry of fairytale fragments; *Love From Kew* is an imaginative scrapbook of scribbled postcard stories. Sophie lives in London. She likes mudlarking and mountains.

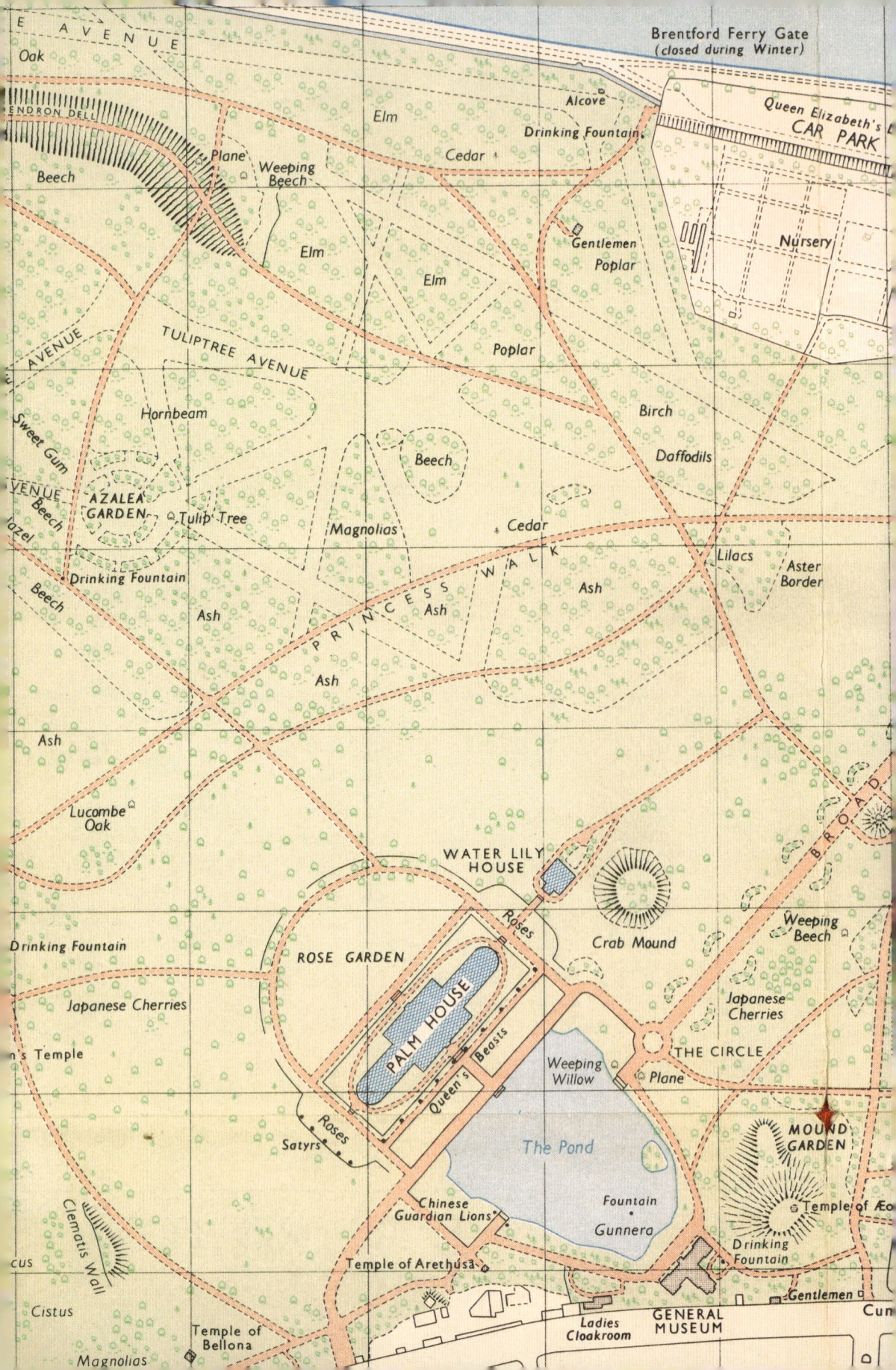